Mickey Mantle:

Inside and Outside the Lines

Tom Molito

BLACK ROSE writing™

ISBN: 978-1-61296-687-8
PUBLISHED BY BLACK ROSE WRITING
www.blackrosewriting.com

Printed in the United States of America
Suggested retail price $15.95

Mickey Mantle: Inside and Outside the Lines is printed in Adobe Caslon Pro
Cover Image credited to Marvin E. Newman, Photographer, 1956

My book is dedicated to my wife of almost 40 years, Kathleen, who has been my North Star.

Special Thanks and Love to Christine, Luke and Laura-Anne; great children, great adults.

Thank You P.J., John and Elisa; my children couldn't have married more quality folks.

To Natalie, Caroline & Hilary, my Grandkids who I learn from every day.

Thanks "Doc" Friend, a real friend and researcher and editor supreme. I'm sure you're up there with Babe, Lou, Joe & Mickey.

Thanks Charlie Daniels' a Patriot and peerless Entertainer. You the best Hoss!

To Denise Bucci Iobbi an indispensable friend.

To David Anderson and Richard Baranowski; gone but not forgotten.

To "Taz" DiGregorio and Tommy Crain of the Charlie Daniels Band; miss you, Rock On!

Praise for *Mickey Mantle: Inside and Outside the Lines*

"Tom Molito grew up a New York Yankee fan and along with many other New Yorkers and others throughout the U.S., a huge Mickey Mantle fan. This book not only shows how fortunate Molito was to have a personal relationship with Mantle, but he also adds some great background information on Mantle's life and career." –Chuck Barksdale, *Mostly Fiction*

"Molito touches on the important moments, good and bad, in Mantle's career, from his quick ascension to the majors, to his almost immediate slow decline in health after reaching the pinnacle of his career. He delves deeply why Mantle was so beloved, how so many people hung on his every at bat, and how in his prime, however fleeting that moment was, he was almost superhuman is his ability to play baseball. I found myself laughing out loud several times. Definitely a book to read and enjoy." –Edwin Howard, *Goodreads reviewer*

"Interesting and a unique writing style." –Sean Talbot, *Sean's Book Reviews*

"Are you a Mickey fan? A Yankee fan? A baseball fan? If you answer yes to any of these questions, then you will love this book. This is a great, easy read about Mantle on and off the field. I've read a number of books on Mantle and found I got a fresh new understanding of the man and player. I wish I got to see him play, but may just be seeing that in (Bryce) Harper." –Brian Rothbart, *NetGalley Professional Reader*

"Nice easy read. Good concise review of both Mantle the person and Mantle the player." –Edward Skwiersky, *Amazon Top Reviewer*

Mickey Mantle:

Inside and Outside the Lines

So they prayed as AJAX harnessed himself in burnished, gleaming bronze and once he strapped his legs and chest in amour, out he marched like the giant god of battle.

The Iliad as translated by Fragle

Several years before Mantle entered the Betty Ford Clinic in January 1994, his friend Tom Molito, a videographer, would film him at a particularly liquid New York banquet. When Mantle was shown the footage by Molito in an effort to compel his friend to confront his addiction, he was furious. "I asked him if he had ever met Elvis," Molito said. "He didn't understand why I asked."

Sports Illustrated, October 11, 2010

FOREWORD

By Charlie Daniels: Three-Time Grammy Winning Country Rock legend

To me, Mickey Mantle was a figure bigger than life that I remember so well from the World Series of my youth. He was a hero in pinstripes on black-and-white TV who was apt to put one over the fence anytime he stepped to the plate.

In those days, if someone had told me I would someday meet Mickey, I would have thought they had been imbibing some of the locally produced white lightning. I would have felt that I had just as good a chance of meeting the Queen of England.

When my friend Tom Molito was running *Cabin Fever Entertainment*, somehow they pulled it off for the Charlie Daniels Band to play a concert after a Yankees' game. Who introduced us? None other than the legendary slugger himself, Mickey Mantle.

I think Mickey was always a country boy at heart. He loved country music and never lost his Oklahoma accent.

I ran into Mickey a few more times during the years, but the thing I remember most vividly took place just a short time before he died. I had written a song called, "Same Ole Me," and had mentioned in it the names of some of my heroes, Mickey included.

He called me and said, something to the effect that, "You need to get that John Wayne stuff out of your song." I said, "Well, who should I use?" He replied, "Just me."

That's the last time I talked to the great Mickey Mantle, and it's good to know he never lost his sense of humor … I'm glad my buddy, Tom Molito, has shared his heartfelt memories.

Charlie Daniels
October 13, 2014

"SAME OL' ME"
(Charlie Daniels, Craig Wiseman, Blue Hat Music)
Well I've been around for a year or two
I guess I'm redneck white and blue
But I ain't nothing but a hard working simple man
I like dogs and railroad trains
Mickey Mantle and ol' John Wayne
I'm a Tennessee Vol and a Dallas Cowboy fan

Chorus:

I'm gonna saw my fiddle and sing about the little man
I'm gonna wave them stars and stripes every time I can
I'm gonna keep my guns and have my fun and call 'em
just the way I see
It's a brand new world but I'm still the same ol'me

INTRODUCTION

I am in a cult that is increasing in membership with the passage of time, which is exceptional. I'm one of the millions of baby boomers who was mesmerized by Mickey Mantle, the great New York Yankees' center fielder whose legacy is greater today than it was when he was playing. Baseball fans today, thanks in part to modern statistics, have concluded that Mantle was better than those who saw him play realized. Young fans who never saw him play have joined my cult of Mantle addicts and thirst for stories and anecdotes about him, which is where I enter. Everyone is special in some way, and what differentiates me from almost all other Mickey Mantle fans is that my hero became my friend.

What makes "Mantle mania" remarkable is that the children of the 1950s and 1960s have carried Mickey Mantle into their adult lives. I have constantly met folks of my generation who are as impassioned by Number 7 as I am, despite the fact it's almost 50 years since he played his last game. We share memories of our childhood households and how everything stopped when "Mickey came to home plate," usually on a small-screened, black and white television set. Our families didn't know each other, but we had the same conversations in our homes that were usually trigged by "Man, look at that home run," or "Oh, no. I hope the injury isn't serious," or "Do you believe that play?"

The drama of Mickey Mantle batting was like a Shakespearean play. We never knew what would happen, but it was usually dramatic. Would this be the at-bat that produced the first ball ever hit out of Yankee Stadium? Would this at-bat result in a crippling injury that would seriously threaten Mickey's career? We had seen him hit balls off facades and over monuments 500 feet away, and we had seen Mickey in agony, his body betrayed by yet another injury.

From the mid -1980s until his heroic passing in 1995, I was friends with Mickey Mantle. I saw the best of Mickey and sometimes the worst. We shared laughter and tears. At times, my memories of Mickey's playing days were more accurate than his own. One quiet evening, Mickey and I were talking about his 1957 season, which was one of the best any player ever had.

Mickey said to me, "I batted .348." I diplomatically asked, "Wasn't it .365, Mickey?" Mickey merely nodded and I could see that he really didn't think it was very important, but it was. I went from a child who had hero-worshipped this man to a trusted friend who helped him say good-bye to America in 1995.

Mickey Mantle is part of American folklore. As with the Kennedy's, Elvis Presley and Marilyn Monroe, the stories, triumphs, tragedies, images and legendary events have been passed on to the next generation. Mention Mickey Mantle and the mythology surfaces. Huck Finn comes to the Big City with matchless raw baseball skills. He has suffered and will suffer crippling injuries, being booed by fans and then being worshipped by the same fans. He will tarnish his image by his drinking and then redeem his legacy with his valiant final message.

During May 1994, *Sports Illustrated* ran a cover story on Mickey, which was an autobiographical confession centered on his alcoholism. The article was filled with regrets concerning Mickey's public and private lives. It was courageous for Mickey to reveal all his flaws, but when I finished the article, I felt that Mickey had been far too hard on himself, and that he still didn't realize what he meant to his fans. I decided to write him a letter and tell him what he meant to me.

I told Mickey that, "I was a little upset by the *Sports Illustrated* article. First of all, Kathleen (my wife) thinks you're much better looking than that terrible cover photograph! But seriously, I thought the article missed one very important point, and that would be, beyond your baseball accomplishments, the happiness and joy you gave to an entire generation of the American public. I don't think you realize that in a world that can be filled with monotony, struggle and heartbreak, following your baseball exploits provided a relief and joy to millions and still does. When I finished your article, I had the feeling that you, Mickey, did not fully comprehend what you mean to people. Trust me. I can't think of more than a handful of Americans whose legacy could simply be, 'He made people happy.'"

Of course, it was even more than that. Every day, sometimes only for a fleeting moment, an image of Mickey, the Yankees, and a young Tom Molito appears in my head. I am once again in my youth, once again watching Mickey hit a home run. I have returned to a wonderful time in the past.

I've told many stories over the years of our friendship. Listeners are usually fascinated. In 2014, at the strong urging of my friend Geoff Orlando, another Mantle fanatic, I decided to commit these memories to paper. This book is for all those kids who never had the chance to double date with Mickey Mantle.

CHAPTER 1

MOUNT OLYMPUS

The front desk manager raised his head and told me to proceed to the house phone. "Dial 870 for Mr. Mantle's room," he said matter of factly. The words had the power of a mantra. *Mickey Mantle's Room.*

Beads of sweat formed on my forehead. My blood pressure jumped so high from the rush of adrenaline that I thought I might collapse. No longer was I a 45-year-old business executive who was cool under pressure. As I hesitatingly approached the phone, the 10-year-old boy whom society forces adults to suppress could no longer be inhibited. I experienced exhilaration and agitation simultaneously and for the first time,

Mickey Mantle had always been my hero during an era of real heroes. Dwight Eisenhower, Albert Einstein, John Wayne, Gary Cooper, Elvis Presley, Chuck Berry and Lucille Ball were icons, but for me, it was Mickey. He was the Yankees' center fielder who hit the ball farther than anyone and he was the fastest runner baseball had ever seen. He possessed a lethal combination of speed and power that baseball scouts only dream about.

Mickey Mantle was the All-American Boy. He was Babe Ruth, Jack Armstrong, and Red Grange wrapped up in one. His platinum blond hair complemented his natural muscular build and boyish good looks. All that was missing was the cape with the big "S." Mickey was 5'11" and about 195 pounds. His shoulders, arms, and back rippled with powerful muscles and his neck was immense. Mickey's forearms equaled those of Popeye the Sailor after Popeye had his fill of spinach, but Mickey's body was racked with injuries, which forced him to play most of his career at a tremendous disadvantage because only the most severe afflictions prevented him from playing.

My first memory of Mickey Mantle was when I saw his picture in the *1952 Yankees Yearbook*. Despite the passage of so many years, I vividly remember the 20-year-old New York Yankee standing out in dramatic contrast to Yankees' grizzly veterans Allie Reynolds, Yogi Berra, Phil Rizzuto, Hank Bauer and Johnny Mize. The Yankees had just won their fourth consecutive World Championship, which tied the 1936-1939 Yankees of Lou Gehrig and Joe DiMaggio, but these Yankees would win one more title to set a record that has never been approached.

Curiously, on one level, I was enjoying the tension the way a poker addict awaiting her next card anticipates gratification but fears defeat. I picked up the telephone and dialed. For an instant, the way a 10-year-old prays his teacher is absent the day of the big test, I almost hoped that no one would answer, but the thought was aborted before it could be fully conceptualized. The voice on the other end said, "Hello, hello," in an unmistakable Oklahoman southern drawl that I had heard hundreds of times in baseball interviews, television appearances and commercials. We all have seen the guy who is so excited that he speaks but words don't come out. I became that person. I was speechless. Nothing came out except, as Ralph Kramden used to say, "Humma, humma."

I finally identified myself as Tom Molito and blurted out something about a video. Mickey replied, "Are you the guy Greer told me we were meeting this morning?" Greer Johnson was Mickey's business agent. I managed to choke out a "Yes," and Mickey instructed me to be in the coffee shop in about 20 minutes.

The host seated me and as I waited, I reflected on my first trip to Yankee Stadium. My dad had taken me to the great ballpark in 1954, his dad had taken him when he was a boy and I had taken my son Luke in the 1980s. Baseball games were not televised in color in the early and mid-1950s, at least not the baseball games I watched. As my dad and I walked through the tunnel that led to the section where we would sit I, like millions of other kids who had come before me, I was dumb struck at the intense rainbow of colors that appeared the instant we exited the ramp into the light.

The aqua blue colored seats, lush green grass, chestnut brown dirt and sparkling white Yankees' uniforms were emblazoned in my memory forever.

The Stadium, with its triple deck grandstand, was like nothing I had ever seen. It conjured up an image of the Roman Coliseum. The pleasing aroma of freshly cut grass, hot dogs, popcorn and beer competed against the smells of cigar and cigarette smoke. It was the perfume of baseball before the era of lattes and wine. The Yankees won, we caught a foul ball, got pitcher Frank "Spec" Shea's autograph and to top it off, Mickey and Yogi each hit a home run.

The appearance of Greer and Mickey jolted me back to the present. It's funny how seeing your hero in person is like not seeing him at all. It was as if a man wearing a buckskin jacket, jeans and cowboy boots with grayish-blond hair barely visible under a black cowboy hat, calling himself Mickey Mantle, was approaching. It was difficult for me to reconcile the fact that the man greeting me was the image that I used to watch on television. I have no idea what Greer was wearing. How could I? I only could see Mickey Mantle.

What I do remember, too strikingly, was Mickey's noticeable limp. It seemed so incongruous. His still magnificent body supported by flawed knees was a disturbing sight. I thought to myself, "What kind of records could he have set with good knees?" Damaged knees and legs prevented Mickey Mantle from being the greatest player of all time, but he may have become the most beloved. A national magazine, upon Mickey's retirement after the 1968 season, commented that "Mickey was cheered more than any American since General Douglas MacArthur after World War II."!

Greer Johnson had been a schoolteacher in North Carolina with a southern drawl that rivaled Mickey's. She was all lady with a shrewd business sense. As she and Mickey sat down, Greer didn't waste any time. "Let's talk about the deal."

Well," I offered, "I'm probably the 10,000[th] person who's come to you with a business proposition." I was well aware that Mickey had been notoriously exploited early in his career by deals proposed by "slickers," as he called them. I outlined the concept of Mickey hosting a one-hour video program involving the then-current 14 players who had hit at least 500 career home runs. Before the shadow of performance-enhancing substances reared its ugly head, the 500 Home Run Club was the measure of true Hall of Fame worthy sluggers. I pointed out that Mickey's popularity cut across generations, making him the most popular of all players. Having Mickey

Mantle host a show about the other great home run hitters was a natural.

Mickey seemed agreeable. Greer and I had discussed financial details earlier that week on the phone after the Yankees' publicity director had willingly told me how to contact her, with the proviso that the project would be produced at Yankee Stadium and must include, of course, a fee for the Yankees.

As our discussion continued, the clincher occurred when I mentioned that Mickey's co-host would be nationally renowned sportscaster Bob Costas. Mickey and Bob had worked together before and Mickey trusted him, which was important. Bob Costas was no different from millions of other grown men, even famous ones, whose hero was Mickey Mantle. Known primarily for his television work, Costas is a multi-award winning baseball traditionalist. He still carries a baseball card of Mickey Mantle in his wallet, which he refers to as "a religious artifact."

I think that I made my first real connection with Mickey when I mentioned that I loved country music and was on the Board of the Country Music Association in Nashville. We recollected that our grandfathers had turned us on to country music. Mickey and I loved Gene Autry, Tex Ritter, Patsy Cline and Tennessee Ernie Ford. I promised to send him some of my company's country music videos, which got me points. We made small talk as I valiantly attempted to remain business-like.

Mickey charged the meal to his room and thankfully didn't comment on the fact that I hadn't touched a morsel. I hoped he didn't realize I was too wound up to eat, but he probably did. Now, I had eaten in luxurious restaurants before and had attended many business meetings with power executives and celebrities. Eating, as my wife has said many times, is not one of my problems, but this was different. I mean, I was involved in a business venture with Mickey Mantle.

As we were getting ready to leave, two well-dressed businessmen passed our table. They had been "eye-balling" Mickey and were nervous as they hesitatingly asked if they could say hello and shake his hand. As I spent more and more time with Mickey, I learned that this was a familiar ritual. Regardless of their status, fans were nervous, dumbstruck and a little starry-eyed in the presence of Mickey Mantle. It's a characteristic of most baseball fans that grew up in the 1950s and 1960s.

As we parted, I told Mickey and Greer that I would send them a script for their review. Driving home on the Major Deegan Expressway, I passed Yankee Stadium, but this time it was different. I had always identified with the Yankees. When they won, I won. When they lost, I lost. It's a feeling that is common among baseball fans, but now when I saw Yankee Stadium, it was more than that. I thought of the first game that I attended in 1954 and of the meeting with Mickey and Greer a little earlier. I was going to be partners with Mickey Mantle. We were going to be on the same team. I couldn't hit, I couldn't throw, and I couldn't field, but it didn't matter because in this game, they were not the necessary skills.

CHAPTER 2

BEGINNINGS

My childhood bedroom was like some hidden cave with ancient hieroglyphics and paintings. Every inch of my Yonkers, New York bedroom was covered with magazine photographs, newspaper clippings, and baseball cards of Mickey Mantle. I remember the room graphically, but not only because of the decorated walls. There were hot water steam pipes on the lower right side of my bed and during the night, as I was sleeping, I would be shockingly awakened if my toes brushed against the pipes. Why the bed wasn't moved is one of the mysteries of my childhood. My younger brother Ed and I shared the room, which meant that he had to share the Mantle motif. When I left for the service in 1966, Ed converted the room into a rock and roll, psychedelic, lights flashing, painted black, "cool" place. I'm certain that my mother would have preferred printed floral patterns to Mickey Mantle and later Jimi Hendrix themes.

Baseball entered my life at an early age. My Sicilian grandfather "Mac," a second generation Italian American, had played baseball in the early 20th century and maintained his powerful body, sculptured by the demands of his stone mason job. "Mac" played baseball in the Laconia section of the Bronx for a team called the Violets. The Violets were a tough team and it would not have been an exaggeration to refer to the them as the "Violent Violets," since they always bet their opponents $10 on the game's outcome and, on the rare occasions that they lost, they fought with the opposition.

My dad was a fan and enjoyed watching the Yankees on our black and white TV. It was my Uncle Chubby -- yes he was called Chubby even though he was slim -- who really jump-started my love of baseball. He told tales of how he used to perform neighborhood household chores in the morning in order to earn the admission to the bleachers. For 55 cents, he got to watch Lou Gehrig and Joe DiMaggio turn Bronx soil into hallowed, sacred ground. Chubby had played baseball at Columbia University and inherited Gehrig's position, first base. As a child, he had met and actually had shaken hands with Babe Ruth at my grandfather's summer home in Peekskill, New York. So, the pump was primed. Call it brainwashing or folklore -- I was a New York Yankees fan.

Joe DiMaggio was the Zeus among the Yankee gods. Considering my family's Italian background, it would have been heresy not to adore DiMaggio, and to bestow Phil Rizzuto, Yogi Berra, Frank Crosetti, Vic Raschi and Tony Lazzeri choice positions in "the family," but I must admit that there was one player I followed religiously through box scores who wasn't even a New York Yankee.

Reno Bertoia played for the Detroit Tigers, the Washington Senators (who became the Minnesota Twins) and the Kansas City A's. He is one of only six major leaguers born in Italy. Among that select group is Rugger Ardizoia, from Oleggio, Italy, who pitched two innings and wore number 14 for the 1947 Yankees. Reno Bertoia was primarily a third baseman who could play second base and shortstop. He didn't hit much, as his .244 lifetime batting average reveals, but he had his moments. Reno's career highlight was getting a single, two walks and scoring two runs against Whitey Ford on opening day at Yankee Stadium in 1961 for the Minnesota Twins. Reno was one of my favorites.

It was easy to be awed by Mickey Mantle. He hit with more power than any player since the days of Babe Ruth and Jimmy Foxx and he was faster going from home plate to first base than anyone who had ever played the game. Mantle's combination of power and speed remained despite a myriad of injuries, especially to his knees. The army classified him 4F because of those knees.

Stephen Jay Gould analyzed Mickey's great appeal in the December 1986 issue of *Sport Magazine*. Gould was not a sportswriter. He was an outstanding, controversial evolutionary biologist whose hero was Joe DiMaggio. Gould wrote one of the most fascinating books connecting baseball, evolution and statistics titled, *Full House: The Spread of Excellence from Plato to Darwin*. While Gould considered DiMaggio the model of excellence, he believed that Mickey was a worthy successor and stated compelling reasons for Mickey's appeal.

"Mantle was young, handsome and bristling with talent. His skills satisfied both sides of the great nature/nurture debate, for he combined the struggle of Horatio Alger with the muscles of John Henry. Mantle was the gullible and naïve farm boy who prevailed by good will and bodily strength in a tough world. His country innocence met the Big Apple. Mickey hit New York, symbol of immensity, rapacity, and sophistication at age 19, yet this conjunction of unparalleled talent and naiveté alone in the big city cannot in itself set an enduring legend. Mythological heroes need flaws and tragedies."

Those who followed Mickey Mantle, during or after his career, are well aware of the flaws and tragedies that befell him. Some were genetically unavoidable, some were self-imposed and some were created by circumstances. Mickey Mantle was no less human than you or I.

Mickey Mantle was going to be the next Joe DiMaggio. The 19-year-old switch-hitting shortstop had batted .383 for Class C Joplin in 1950, and as early as January 6, 1951, legendary baseball writer Roscoe McGowan wrote that a possible replacement for DiMaggio was Mickey Mantle. Tom Greenwade, the scout who discovered Mickey and who helped persuade the Brooklyn Dodgers to bring Jackie Robinson to the big leagues, held the opinion that Mantle was a shortstop who "might be a great center fielder."

Growing up, Mickey worked in the zinc mines with his father, Mutt, earning $35 a week. Mickey once told me how Mutt got him a job cleaning out the area around telephone poles. "You see, when you have a prairie fire, if you don't clean out a 10-yard spot around a telephone pole, it will burn the telephone pole out, and it will cost you a lot of money."

While still in high school, Mantle played semipro baseball for the Baxter Springs Whiz Kids. Tom Greenwade was passing through Baxter Springs, which was just across the state line in Kansas, to scout a player in a nearby town. There was a ballpark besides the road and a game was being played. Greenwade stopped to watch. Mickey hit three home runs that night, two right-handed and one left-handed. The rest is history.

Tom Greenwade was proud of being a New York Yankee. While he was with the Yankees from 1949-64, they won 14 pennants and nine world championships. Greenwade was one of the great scouts when the role involved discovering young talent, not just recommending which players to select in the draft. He was the prototypical baseball scout. In addition to Mantle, Greenwade brought Bobby Murcer, Elston Howard, Hank Bauer, Clete Boyer, Ralph Terry, Tom Sturdivant, Jerry Lumpe, Bill Virdon and

Whitey Herzog to the Yankees. Bunch Greenwade, Tom's son, knew how much his father had contributed to baseball.

"I realize my opinion is biased because he's my dad," said Bunch Greenwade, "but I really feel Dad contributed as much to baseball as a lot of people in the Hall of Fame. Dad put so many people in baseball that wouldn't have been there if Dad hadn't stuck out his neck."

In 1941, Greenwade became a scout for the St. Louis Browns. A few years later, Branch Rickey signed him to scout the Negro Leagues. Bunch explained.

"Dad decided Jackie Robinson had more heart and more physical ability than another player. I know it was no problem for my father to be scouting a black player. You see, his mother died when he was 10 years old, and he had a hard time, but some black friends helped him out and I think he probably put forth extra effort for that reason."

Occasionally, Bunch accompanied his father to scout a player.

"Some scouts take a lot of notes and use a stopwatch to time the runners," Bunch told a reporter. "Dad didn't believe in that. He said, 'I can tell if a player can run or not.' Dad watched for speed, a good eye and a strong arm. If a pitcher didn't throw hard, Dad wasn't interested."

There has been much discussion the last two or three years with respect to who is a "true" Yankee. The concept is not new. One time at a meeting discussing a prospect with general manager George Weiss, Greenwade said, "Mr. Weiss, he just isn't a Yankee." The Yankees didn't sign him and he never made the big leagues.

Near the end of spring training, it had been decided that Mantle *was* the player the Yankees had been seeking to replace the Yankee Clipper when the greatest center fielder who ever played the game retired. Yankees' manager Casey Stengel wasn't certain if Mantle would make the team in 1951, but the switch-hitter would be there whenever DiMaggio left.

Modern fans might not realize the magnitude of pressure brought to bear on Mickey. The Yankees wanted him play for Binghamton, which was a notch above Joplin in the minor league hierarchy, but once Mantle displayed his skills and vast potential, Binghamton was out. The question was whether he would play for Triple A Kansas City or for the Yankees.

Unlike today, it was rare for young players, no matter how spectacular, to jump to the big team with so little minor league experience, but Mantle seemed to be different. Almost all the experts, many of whom were quite conservative in lavishing praise on untried youngsters, raved effusively about Mantle's future. The fact that he was a switch-hitter who was equally adept from either side of the plate merely added to the aura and to the pressure.

But there was a bigger problem than where Mickey Mantle would play baseball. North Korea and South Korea were at war, a war that, to this day, has not officially ended. The United States supported South Korea with troops in what is called the Korean Conflict. Mickey Mantle might be drafted.

On April 3, 1951 Mickey, hitting a robust .462 in the exhibition season, was ordered to report to his draft board for a medical re-examination. Mantle had been classified as 4-F due to osteomyelitis of his left shin, which was the result of a high school football injury incurred in 1946. For a time, the doctors treating Mickey feared that the leg might have to be amputated, but his family refused to consider that horrifying option. After several operations and treatment with the new wonder drug, penicillin, the condition was arrested. Now Mickey's draft board would perform another evaluation. Before the examination, Mantle told reporters that he wouldn't mind going into the army if his leg were okay. "I hope they find out that it is good." It wasn't.

Sometimes, what appears to be a benefit is not. The disease prevented Mickey from serving in the army, but it allowed him to play for the Yankees as a raw 19-year-old. His rookie season that had more than its share of frustration, but Mickey's osteomyelitis also prevented him from becoming as great as his genes would have allowed.

Whitey Ford, who grew up in Queens and was nicknamed "Slick," relates how shy and inarticulate Mickey was when he first reported to the team. "Everything he owned was in a straw suitcase," he said. "No money, none of those $400 suits he got around to buying a couple of years later. Just those two pairs of pastel slacks and that blue sports coat that he wore every place."

Mickey's shyness sheds light on his relationship with Joe DiMaggio. He was so insecure that he would try to avoid DiMaggio. The two played next to each other in the outfield, but Mickey was too awed to even talk to DiMaggio. "Joe DiMaggio was my hero, but he couldn't talk to me because I wouldn't even look at him, although he was always nice and polite."

As my childhood years turned to teen years and slowly into adulthood, I never outgrew Mickey. Few of us did. As I matured, so too did Mickey. I followed his first few seasons as closely as possible and voraciously read everything I could about him. Most of the baseball writers kept waiting for Mickey to finally break out with a memorable season that would validate his potential. So did I.

I was 12 during the wondrous 1956 season when the baton from Ruth and DiMaggio was officially passed to Mickey Mantle, who not only won the Triple Crown, but also led the major leagues in almost every offensive category. In addition to hitting 52 home runs, he drove in 130 runs, slugged over .700, scored 132 times and recorded 79 extra base hits. The performance was comparable to DiMaggio's and even Ruth's greatest seasons. Mickey Mantle was clearly the best player in the game.

My interactions with Mickey Mantle had consisted of seeing him from the far reaches of Yankee Stadium or seeing an image on our black-and-white TV set. At the Stadium, my friends and I would constantly try to sneak into the box seats, only to be repeatedly told to "get back and out" by the red-uniformed, elderly ushers of a by-gone era.

The final out of the game would trigger a fast paced walk to the fenced parking lot across the street from the Yankees' executive offices, where the cars of the Yankees' players, in some cases with their drivers, would be waiting for the arriving heroes (or occasionally, goats). In the 1950s and 1960s, most of the Yankees traveled to Northern New Jersey to their in-season homes.

Eventually, Mickey would come out and walk beyond police barricades to his car and driver. He was always one of the last players to leave the locker room. Knowledgeable Yankees fans knew that Mickey's removing the tape he used on his legs before every game was a time consuming, painstaking job.

I distinctly remember waiting in the rain one night for the appearance of Number 7. It is amazing how 30 seconds, one half of a minute, has remained etched in my memory. I don't recall which family member drove me to this game, but looking back, whoever it was could have easily and justifiably denied my request to wait such a long time in order to see Mickey dash into his car on a rainy night, but he or she didn't and I saw Mickey Mantle up-close.

Mickey gave the fans a tight-lipped smile, but something else struck me. I sensed a trace of fear. In this pre-paparazzi era, Mickey's well-intentioned fans were a little scary as they shoved pens, cards, baseballs and other items in his face. Celebrities such as Mickey, Ali, Willie Mays and later Michael Jordan could not appear in public without attracting a throng of admirers.

Many years later Mickey would relate that he sometimes felt like a prisoner because he often was forced to remain in his hotel room to avoid screaming fans. He made sure to mention that he understood them, but that sometimes he wished he could be treated like anyone else.

At that time in my life, our seats were usually the upper tier grandstand, which was fine. Still, I've often thought that on some level, an individual's current status in life could be judged on where he sat at Yankee Stadium. The better you did financially and the more influential people you knew translated into better seats. I took great satisfaction in moving from the upper tier in left field to choice box seats or even a luxury box on occasion when I became a successful business man, but part of me missed the earlier times when I still could look forward to the day that I would be able to afford to pay for any seat at the Stadium instead of having to sneak past an usher.

I have an almost-wonderful memory of sitting high in the third deck behind the left field foul pole during the seventh game of the 1957 World Series. It would have been truly wonderful but the game was a disappointment since the Yankees lost to the Milwaukee Braves. I still don't like Lew Burdette or Eddie Mathews.

Burdette, who once had been with the Yankees, won three games in that Series, while Mathews won the fourth game with a three run, 10th inning home run to tie the Series. With each team having two wins, the fifth game was pivotal. Neither team scored until the bottom of the sixth inning, when Mathews beat out a slow ground ball to the right side that second baseman Jerry Coleman didn't charge. Mathews was credited with a single, Henry Aaron singled him to third and Joe Adcock singled to score Mathews with the game's only run as Burdette shutout the Yankees. Coleman apologized for his gaff after the game as Yankees' starter Whitey Ford comforted Coleman by reminding him that you have to score to win.

The best part of the day had been before the game because it was really great being with my uncle Chubby and grandfather Mac. We had lunch in a small establishment called Kelley's, located on Babe Ruth Plaza. I'm not sure if they ate, since the place was, in reality, a bar that served lunch. The interior was green, wood paneled, and dark. There were large black and white photographs of all the Yankees' immortals on the walls ---Ruth, Gehrig, Dickey, DiMaggio and Mickey. The mixed aroma of beer, smoke and hot pastrami permeated the air. I've been to four-star restaurants that were very nice, but the experience of being in them is not burned into my memory like

Kelley's on Babe Ruth Plaza, just off the Grand Concourse.

My uncle Chubby, grandfather Mac and I got into our seats located in the upper deck near the left field foul pole about an hour before the start of the game. Racing through my mind endlessly was the fact that it was the seventh game of the 1957 World Series. It made me very nervous. Uncle Chubby asked me if I wanted anything to eat. The thought of food made me nauseous.

The Yankees were taking batting practice. I refused to watch them hit because I didn't want to use up all the home runs they were hitting. I wanted to see them when they counted, which reminded me of the belief that a hitter has a limited number of good swings and a pitcher has a limited number of throws in his arm.

Mickey wasn't supposed to play. Milwaukee Braves second baseman Red Schoendienst had fallen on Mickey's right shoulder on a pick off play, forcing both of them out the fourth game, but this was the seventh game of the World Series. When I learned that Mickey would play, I was much more confident.

Warren Spahn, who was scheduled to start, had the flu, which forced Milwaukee Braves' manager Fred Haney to replace him with Lew Burdette, who had pitched a shutout in Game 5 on two days' rest. It is not possible that that would have happened today.

It was difficult to gauge the strike zone from where we were sitting, a reality that didn't stop the fans near me from helping home plate umpire Bill McKinley make his calls. The Braves went down in order in the first. Our lead-off hitter Hank Bauer, the gritty ex-Marine, hit Burdette's first pitch for a double. The tension welled up again. The Yankees had to score. They didn't.

I knew there was trouble when Enos Slaughter hit a come backer to the mound. Bauer was hung up between second and third. He returned safely to second as the aggressive Slaughter rounded first base with his head down. He was tagged out, bringing up Mickey. All the Mick could do was hit a soft ground ball back to Burdette for the second out.

I was really upset because I knew that we had to get to Burdette when we had the chance. Uncle Chubby hit his knee with his fist in disgust. I was afraid to look at my grandfather. The Yankees were great against fast ball pitchers, but Burdette threw a sinker that every Yankee, to a man, thought was a spitball. The Yankees had class and didn't use that as an excuse.

Mickey, a great hitter, was followed by Yogi Berra in the order. It is no denigration to Mantle to point out that opponents feared Berra as much as Mickey. After Mickey had grounded out, Haney ordered an intentional walk to Yogi. He knew how important it was to score first.

Gil McDougald was the batter. He never was the same hitter after his line drive up the middle hit Herb Score in the eye earlier that season. Haney made the right move as McDougald popped up to end the threat. Then I really got sick in the third inning.

Larsen retired Burdette on a foul pop up behind third, but Hazle, going the other way, hit a single to left. The Yankees lost the World Series when Johnny Logan hit a scorching grounder to third base that looked like a certain double play. Tony Kubek fielded it cleanly and fired to Jerry Coleman at second, but Kubek's throw pulled Coleman off the bag. Coleman fired to first in an attempt to get at least one out. Too late. Logan beat the throw, putting Braves at first and second with one out.

I kept repeating to Chubby and Mac, "The inning should be over, the inning should be over." But it was just starting. Eddie Mathews drove in Hazle and Logan with a double down the right field line, Bobby Shantz came in for Larsen, the Braves scored two more runs and I was crestfallen.

As we left the ballpark, the joy and excitement of watching the seventh game of the World Series was gone. Chubby asked Mac and me if we wanted to get something to eat before we drove home to Yonkers. I told him that I didn't mind if we went to the Roxy Deli, but I wasn't hungry. I didn't eat until breakfast the next day.

In 1957, actually meeting Mickey Mantle was beyond the wildest dreams of everyone in my neighborhood, yet it seemed as if there was always a chance of it happening because Yogi Berra's attorney, Yugo Antonucci, who was a business partner of my sister's father-in-law, lived a few blocks from my childhood Yonkers home. Yugo, my sister's father-in-law and Yogi were involved in Yogi's successful bowling alley venture. Unlike Yogi, for whom every business deal seemed to turn to gold, Mickey had no business sense. He finally became involved with lawyer Roy True, who provided Mickey with the proper business focus. I would occasionally stare at the Antonucci house, thinking out loud, "Maybe Mickey's there with Yogi." We never saw anyone, but it added a touch of excitement to the neighborhood.

Five years later, in 1961, I was a 17-year-old, captivated by the great Home Run Race between Mickey, Roger Maris, and Babe Ruth. In all lives, there are "what-ifs?" They were a major theme in not only Mickey's personal life, but also in his career. If Mickey hadn't suffered a leg ailment late in the 1961 season, the results of the home run race might have ended dramatically differently.

Nineteen sixty-one was the greatest baseball season of my life, although I must admit that I have since been seduced by the 1998 Yankees. David Cone, David Wells, Derek Jeter, Mariano, El Duque, Tino, Bernie, and the rest of the that great 1998 cast won more games than the 1961 team. From a purely personal perspective, I was young in 1961 and Mickey Mantle was in center field, which is why for me, it's 1961.

The Yankees started out slowly that season, losing on opening day to the Minnesota Twins, 6-0 (remember Reno Bertoia?). Mickey went hitless in four at-bats with two strikeouts as Pete Ramos limited the Yankees to three measly singles. I was disappointed and after only one game, I questioned new Yankees' manager statement in spring training that Mickey would be the team leader. Yes, I'm a typical Yankees' fan.

There's a revealing sidelight to the story. After the season, Mickey made an admission that many athletes are too proud to acknowledge.

"... Ralph Houk came along and changed my whole idea of thinking about myself. I still didn't have a lot of confidence. Not till Houk came along and told me, 'You are going to be my leader. You're the best we've got.'"

After the opening day loss, the Yankees reeled off five straight wins. At the end of April, they trailed the first place Detroit Tigers by a game, but when the weather warmed up, so did Mickey and Roger Maris. I remember how I couldn't wait for the games to start to see Mickey or Roger or both hit a home run. The first game of a twilight doubleheader at the Stadium in late July against the White Sox was a template for the season.

I didn't get home until the game was in the bottom of the fourth inning because the first game of the doubleheader started at 5:30. I turned on the television and to this day, I can still hear Yankees' broadcaster Mel Allen saying, "Wall to wall home runs. Roger Maris' three-run blast hit the right field foul pole and Mickey Mantle has just hit the left field foul pole. How about that?"

Mickey had one of his best seasons. He had a great shot at Babe Ruth's single season home run record, but once again, an injury got in the way. The Yankees swept a three game series at the Stadium from the Tigers at the beginning of September and coasted the rest of the way on their way to the pennant as the Tigers collapsed. The focus was now completely on the home run chase between Mantle, Maris and Ruth. Soon it would be only Maris against Ruth.

Mantle had the flu in September, or so he thought. Yankees' broadcaster Mel Allen referred Mickey to his general practitioner, Dr. Max Jacobson, who administered a flu shot to Mickey's hip. It was a terrible decision because an abscess developed on Mickey's upper leg, effectively ending his season. During the 1970s, Dr. Jacobson lost his medical license because his actions led to several patient fatalities.

Mickey batted only six times in the 1961 World Series against the Cincinnati Reds, hitting a key single in the fourth inning of the fourth game that led to the game's first run. As Mickey rounded first base, everyone in the ballpark gasped in horror at his bloodstained uniform. The wound on his infected hip had opened. That was it, of course. Ralph Houk sent in Hector Lopez to run for Mickey as the Yankees went on to win, 7-0. Curt Schilling wasn't the first player to bleed in the World Series.

I was really dismayed. Mickey didn't get the chance to break Ruth's single season home run record and now he would miss the rest of the World Series. So many things went through my mind when I saw Mickey trot back to the dugout. My hero had suffered yet another injury that might have been prevented if he hadn't taken the flu shot. His World Series performance the year before against the Pirates had been exceptional as the Yankees lost a Series they were supposed to win. Some of my friends who rooted against the Yankees never let me forget it. We couldn't afford to lose this Series to the Reds. I tried to think about Monday afternoon when the next game would be played.

The Yankees beat the Reds in the fifth game to win their 19th World Championship in a World Series that was much closer than the box scores indicate. In the fifth game, the Yankees' outfield consisted of Johnny Blanchard in right field, Hector Lopez in left and Roger Maris in center. I was relieved that there would be no need for a sixth game.

A year earlier, during the summer of 1960, I was 16 and working in construction when I heard a familiar whistle. It was my grandfather "Mac." He had arranged for me to take the rest of the day off and handed me a ticket to the All-Star game that was being played *that* afternoon, Wednesday, July 13, at Yankee Stadium. It would be the first All-Star game in the Bronx since 1939 and only the second in the history of the Stadium.

During the 1950s and 1960s, the All-Star game was meaningful. Inter-league play and free agency, two prime movers that contributed greatly to the American and National Leagues losing their identities, was decades away. Ticket sales for the game at the Stadium lagged well behind expectations. The Yankees announced that bleacher tickets priced at $2.10 and general admission tickets priced at $4.20 would go on sale at the Stadium the day of the game. Paid attendance was a disappointing 38,362.

As I think back, I cannot help but be amazed that tickets didn't go on sale until the weekend before the game. Box and reserved seats could be purchased in advance, while general admission and bleacher tickets were available only on the day of the game.

It was a humid, uncomfortable 88 degrees on game day. To me, all that mattered were the great players that I would see. The American League starters included Yankees Whitey Ford pitching, Mickey Mantle and Roger Maris in the outfield, Yogi Berra catching and Bill Skowron at first base. Ted Williams, Al Kaline, Luis Aparicio, Nellie Fox, Brooks Robinson and Early Wynn were other American Leaguers. From that impressive array of talent, only Roger Maris and Bill Skowron are not in the Hall of Fame.

The National League had a pretty good team as well. It was the first time that New Yorkers could see National Leaguers since the Brooklyn Dodgers and the New York Giants had left after the 1957 season.

The starting outfield consisted of Willie Mays in center field, Henry Aaron in right field and Bob Skinner in left field. Roberto Clemente pinch-hit in the eighth inning. Stan Musial, Eddie Mathews, Orlando Cepeda, Ernie Banks, Ken Boyer and Bill Mazeroski were other greats on the roster. Only Boyer is not a Hall of Famer. Looking back, I am so grateful to "Mac" for giving me the ticket. I felt good that Mickey clearly was a standout.

Stan Musial had been selected to the National League's squad despite the first sub-par offensive season of his career. St. Louis Cardinals' manager Solly Hemus had the temerity to actually bench Musial at the end of June, which led some "experts" to claim that sentiment had played a role in Musial's selection.

National League manager Walt Alston, who had managed the Dodgers in Brooklyn before Los Angeles stole one of Brooklyn's most prized possessions, admitted that it was true. He didn't care because Alston knew that Musial almost always rose to the occasion. The only Brooklyn manager to win a World Series spoke.

"Sure sentiment entered into it. He is the kind of man I'd like to have around if a situation develops in the ballgame where a big hit could win the game."

One thing that New Yorkers, especially those from Brooklyn knew was that it wasn't smart to underestimate Stanley Frank Musial. In the seventh inning, Musial pinch-hit for pitcher Stan Williams. Facing former teammate Gerry Staley, Musial hit a prodigious home run into the upper deck in right field, increasing the National League's lead to 4-0. It was his sixth All-Star game home run, which broke his own record.

Musial had told baseball writer Harold Kaese that he had a feeling he would hit a home run.

"I thought I would hit a home run today. I had that certain feeling. Remember the all-star game I won with a home run in Milwaukee. I had the feeling that day too."

Stan Musial's first appearance at Yankee Stadium since 1943 brings to mind a little known event that occurred when Mickey Mantle first joined the Yankees in 1951. Mickey told me the story a few years after we became friends.

We were sitting in Mickey's hotel room at the Regency in New York, being relaxed by the liquids in our glasses when Mickey said offhandedly,

"Tom I'm going to tell something that the Yankees made me do. When I came up in 1951, a guy from some paper asked me who was my favorite player. I told him Stan Musial. Well, the Yankees didn't like that at all. They said that I had to say that Joe DiMaggio was my favorite player."

Mickey grew up in Oklahoma and the Cardinals were the closest team. He used to listen to the Cards on the radio when Musial was having some of his "Mickey Mantle seasons." Actually, to be fair, maybe Mickey had some Stan Musial seasons.

Time passed much too quickly. The Yankees declined after winning the 1962 World Series and although they won pennants in 1963 and 1964 to complete their second skein of five consecutive American League Championships (1949-1953 and 1960-1964), there would be hard times ahead. There were no pennants until 1976 and no World Championship until 1977, when Reggie Jackson arrived to help Thurman Munson beat the Los Angeles Dodgers.

In 1966, a bad year for the Yankees but Mickey's last decent season (.288 with 23 home runs in only 108 games due to injuries), I graduated from Iona

College in New Rochelle. I had put myself through college by working during the summer in construction. It was backbreaking work, which served as great motivation to complete my education. Tuition was only $600 a semester and I remember my father providing money so I didn't have to work during one particularly frigid Winter Recess.

After graduation, I was drafted and spent Mickey's final two seasons, 1967 and 1968, in the U.S. Army. I was assigned to the 146th Infantry Brigade in Fort Hood, Texas. The barracks leader, Sgt. Moore, an enlisted E-8 "lifer," was responsible for compiling the lists of men who would go to Southeast Asia. Fortunately, my grandfather had given me an old, green DeSoto, which provided me with some freedom while in Texas.

Sgt. Moore didn't drive, which turned out to be a break for me since I had transportation. He conscripted my old green DeSoto and me to take his clothes to the cleaners, to run errands and to perform other sundry tasks. These chores kept my name off the Vietnam lists he created. He would often tell me, in his thick, syrupy, Arkansas drawl, to "keep that fucking car running Yankee!" When not running errands, I was the battalion's mail clerk. Even today, my kids laugh at my wartime mailman status.

I still followed the Yankees' games through the box scores carried in most newspapers. They were seasons Mickey and I would like to forget. Mickey appeared in 144 games each year, but he was no longer the Mickey Mantle we knew. He hit only .245 in 1967 and an even worse .237 in 1968. In retrospect, they were not as bad as they seemed according to Bill James and the sabermetricians.

Pitching dominated during the late 1960s. In 1968, Carl Yastrzemski was the only American League player to bat at least .300 as he won the batting title with a .301 mark. The league batting average was a paltry .230, so I took consolation in the fact that Mickey didn't do that badly.

When I was discharged from the army in 1969, I worked for Nestle for about three years. I took pride in my movement up the corporate ladder of America as I slowly realized it was not what I wanted. My father had been forced to hold two jobs and I remember him wearily dragging himself home from his six day a week sales job. At times, he had to work evenings. My father often was so tired that he seemed so content to sit in his easy chair and watch whatever happened to be on the television screen. Would that happen to me? No, it wouldn't.

Working at Nestle opened up an entirely new world to me. Until that time, I had been around people whose economic and social backgrounds were similar to mine. Even the college I attended, Iona in New Rochelle, consisted primarily of lower and middle class students from New York City's outer boroughs. In the army, as a private in an infantry unit, I was stationed with guys from the same economic and social strata.

Nestle was different. For the first time, I was exposed to co-workers who came from "old money," who were primarily "W.A.S.P.s," and who were part of a "lucky sperm club." They spoke differently, carried themselves with an air of confidence (sometimes false) based on economic security and dressed in an understated style of elegance. They had first names such as "Clay," "Morgan," and "Whitley."

Initially, I aspired to be like them, which was an error. After several years, I realized that I had to cut my own path. I became the "Rebel" in the marketing department. "Bright guy, but what's with his long hair?" was my M.O. On Friday afternoons, when my resentment toward the company for trying to make me conform all week reached an apex, I'd play a game. There were 500 phone extensions. I'd randomly dial an extension and in a very authoritative voice, ask if "they have the number yet?" Interestingly, most of my victims would blurt out some value -- dollars, pounds, cartons, etc.

Nestle eventually made me an offer I couldn't accept. If I cut my hair, I would be promoted. Perhaps it was the time, 1973, but I felt that if I accepted the offer, I would be compromising something important and I resigned. At that point, the lyrics of rock songs by Cat Stevens, the Moody Blues, and Leonard Cohen, which promoted freedom of expression and individuality, made much more sense to me than what I was exposed to in the corporate world.

Leaving was the right move for two reasons. I had come to grips with who I was and I was at the right place at the right time to meet my future bride, Kathleen. Boy, was I lucky; she had looks, class and smarts! Plus a hippie-streak cultivated by attending college in Colorado and Boston. If all that wasn't enough, more compassion and understanding of children then anyone I've ever met.

I returned working for Uncle Chubby's construction company, having reached the conclusion that philosophically, manual labor was a more honorable way to earn a living than corporate politics, which was about attempting to ascend an imaginary slippery ladder in order to get as close to the top as possible. An attraction of baseball, which is not acknowledged enough, is that making the team is based on ability. You can be the owner's son, but if you can't hit a curve ball, you don't make the team.

An interesting exchange that I never forgot occurred the time I found myself in the middle of Harlem, operating a jackhammer in order to break up a concrete sidewalk. I would break the sidewalk into chunks while an elderly Italian immigrant put them into a wheelbarrow. One day, through his heavy accent, he advised, "Go to college so you don't have to do this."

I looked directly at him and informed him that I had graduated from college and chose to be a laborer.

"You went to college? You don't have to do this? You are really stupid!"

I don't know if he was correct but I eventually returned to the corporate world. We have our values. We also have our needs. Sometimes, we must put ourselves into a position that allows us compromise a little, but try to remain true to our beliefs. After all, I *had* gone to college. As fate would have it, one day I was in the plush penthouse of the advertising agency I worked for, which was located in the Chrysler Building. As I looked through the picture window, I saw a high-rise building being built by my uncle's company. There were several workers with whom I had worked. As I sat among the porcelain cups and crystal glasses, I still had doubts whether my place was in or out of the Chrysler Building.

After going through my "hippie stage" and refusing to cut my hair, I found a company, UST, that accepted the fact that my brain was more important than my hair. I must thank its chairman Louis F. Bantle (strange how "Bantle" was my boss and "Mantle" was my hero) for making this distinction. I was a good marketing man. My time at Nestle had been a great training ground.

During those years, I followed the Yankees fortunes. Without Mickey, it was not the same. When the Yankees won the World Series in 1977 and 1978 it was almost like old times, although I admit that I didn't have the same intensity when I watched those games as I did when Mickey played. Little did I know that I would soon get to meet Mickey, my childhood hero, as a business associate and as a friend.

My marketing degree, business experience and Yonkers street-smarts all came together in the early 1980s when I conceived of and formed *Cabin Fever Entertainment*. The company was a video production and distribution company. Its strategic direction was aimed at "Americana" programming. *Cabin Fever Entertainment* was typical American lifestyle, including

Westerns such as *Lonesome Dove*, country music, motor sports, military documentaries and, of course, baseball.

One of our ideas was a program based on the 14 players who had hit 500 Home Runs. We needed a host. Guess who flashed into my mind? We made some probing phone calls to the Yankees to see if my favorite player was a possibility. My mind started to race. Wow, wouldn't it be something if Mantle agreed! If there is a meeting, I hope I don't die before it takes place.

The Yankees' Public Relations representative gave us Mickey's contact number after my assurance that the Yankees would be part of "the deal."

This was becoming "it." I was about to enter Mickey's fast-lane lifestyle that would eventually lead to a friendship with my lifelong idol. Actually, I had "met" Mickey twice prior to my soon to be face-to-face business meeting. In 1967, we met 33,000 feet above the ground. In 1985, we were at a New York bar where Mickey was watching the now-classic Hearns-Hagler fight. Next to Mickey, I saw another pretty good home run hitter named Roger Maris.

CHAPTER 3

MICKEY AT 33,000 FEET

In December 1967, I was stationed at Fort Hood Texas. My tour of duty was made a little easier by knowing that Elvis Presley had served at Fort Hood (since my mother and I shared a great affection for him). I never met Elvis, but little did I know that I was about to meet Mickey Mantle!

I was a specialist 4th class, in uniform, heading home for Christmas. As I approached the boarding area of an American Airlines flight to New York, I glanced ahead and could not believe what I saw. Sitting alone, waiting to board, was a husky, muscular man reading a newspaper. Even from the back, his distinctive outline could not be mistaken for anyone but Mickey Mantle. It's a good thing I didn't have high blood pressure in those days. My heart raced and my brain produced a little voice: "You have to meet him!" But how?"

When we got on line to board the plane, Mickey was ahead. I was disappointed that my military discount coach seat in the rear of the aircraft would be so far away from Mickey, who would be flying first class, that it would be almost impossible to get to meet him. Boy, was I wrong. Despite the poor logistics, I devised my plan.

I was stationed at Ft. Hood with a career "lifer" named Sergeant Major Kerr, who supposedly was a distant relative of Mickey's. This connection was worth a shot, but I had to be careful and I wanted to be respectful. There were many stories about how fans would not allow Mickey to eat a meal and how he was constantly besieged for autographs while dining. As much as I wanted to meet him, I also wanted to respect his privacy. I didn't want to intrude uninvited. Maybe he had a soft spot for an army uniform.

The Yankees had once played an exhibition game at West Point. After the game, they ate in the giant mess hall and the entire corps of cadets started chanting Mickey's name until he got up and said a few words. Only two other men had ever had this honor—Douglas MacArthur and Dwight Eisenhower. The cadets did allow him to eat without interruption.

I wrote a short note to Mickey explaining that I was in Sgt. Major Kerr's unit, which had also been General George S. Patton's old unit. I would love to just come up and shake his hand. A stewardess took the note to give to him.

My heart started to race again. I could see Mickey's first class seat up the aisle through an opened curtain. The stewardess handed Mickey the note. He took it from her. He read it. After reading it, he turned in his seat and motioned with his right arm for me to come up. I didn't believe it but it was true.

As I made my way up the narrow aisle, all my body parts worked, except my feet had turned into two concrete blocks. I believe the term "deer in the head lights" may have originated at the moment. I reached Mickey's seat, apologized for bothering him and explained that I merely wanted to shake his hand.

While I babbled, he got up and moved to the window seat and told me to sit down. I wish every baseball fan could have experienced the next 45 minutes. Mickey couldn't have been nicer. He asked the flight attendant to bring a drink. Her response was a revealing "Would Mr. Mantle want another scotch?" I sensed that Mickey had excellent relationships with the flight attendants' union. We spoke about baseball, with the emphasis on Mickey Mantle.

In 1967, the Yankees suffered their third consecutive poor season. They won only 72 games to finish in ninth place, 20 games behind the pennant winning Red Sox. Mickey, whose knees prevented him from playing the outfield, was the first baseman. He hit only .245 but drew 107 walks, which indicated that pitchers still feared his power. A proud man, it rankled Mickey that the Yankees and he had fallen so far. I remember him telling me that his offensive production had suffered due not only to his now even more brittle body, but also because pitchers were not throwing him any strikes. "I have no strong hitter batting behind me," he said, "with Yogi, Moose and Elston gone." He explained how pitchers were not hesitant to try to make him chase bad pitches. They were indifferent to walking him.

Mickey asked me what I did when I wasn't in the army. I told him that I had graduated from Iona and then was drafted. "I worked in construction to help get my business degree. I'll probably work for some large company in advertising, but I'm not sure that's what I really want." Mickey identified with the construction work and told me that while he would have liked to have attended college, sons of Oklahoma zinc miners usually didn't do that.

I could tell that Mickey was glad that we were talking, which pleased me. I certainly didn't want to sound like a reporter interviewing him. There was so much I wanted to ask. Here was an opportunity that I would never again have, or at least that's what I thought, but I didn't have to ask Mickey many questions because he started talking. He looked directly at my uniform and said, "You know, I regret not being able to wear that uniform." I was a little shaken but regained my composure quickly enough to say, "Mickey, I would give anything to be able to wear your uniform." Mickey laughed.

I wanted to ask Mickey whether he thought it was tougher facing Gibson or Koufax. He had faced Koufax in the 1963 World Series and Gibson in the 1964 Series. His memory was amazing but I guess that there are many players who remember every hit and strikeout, especially in the World Series.

"I can't pick. They were both tough for me and everyone else. They sure did strike me out a lot. Koufax was lefty and Gibson was a righty, so it was different facing them. I only got one good swing against Koufax the whole Series and it was a home run. I hit a home run against Gibby in the seventh game. Neither one mattered much because we lost both World Series."

It seems unbelievable. Mickey Mantle, the Triple Crown Winner who had hit 52 home runs, was seriously thinking of bunting with runners on first and third and one out in a 2-0 game in the seventh game of the World Series. Hank Bauer was on third and Joe Collins was on first with Mickey at the plate. Mickey didn't bunt. He swung from the heels as always and hit a sharp ground ball to first baseman Gil Hodges, who stepped on the bag and then fired home to Brooklyn catcher Roy Campanella. Bauer was trapped between home and third and was finally tagged out at home by Campy to retire the side.

I asked Mickey about his bunting. "My dad taught me how to bunt. He always told me it was another weapon, but it was my mom who told my dad to keep teaching me to bunt. I was pretty fast and when I went into a slump, I could always try to drag a bunt. I can't do that any more." Ted Williams once said that Mickey could hit .400 every year just bunting.

Our talk turned to Phil Rizzuto.

"Phil helped everyone with learning how to bunt. There was never anybody any better. He kept telling me that if I just faked a bunt it would help me because it would force the third baseman and the first baseman to play in a little closer, which would make it easier to hit a ground ball past them. But it didn't help Phil because he never hit the ball hard."

Since Mickey was so open, I decided that it would be fine to talk about the booing, although I admit I felt a little trepidation.

"Mickey," I said, hesitatingly, "how did you feel when they started to cheer you?" He didn't miss a beat.

The first time they stopped booing me was in 1956, but then I didn't win the Triple Crown the next year. When we did poorly in 1959, they blamed me a lot. When we got Roger, they booed me and cheered him. Then in 1961, they started to boo Roger and cheer me."

I had lived through it in 1961. Booing Mantle stopped for two reasons. First, even Yankees' fans couldn't justify booing Mantle when he was having a season that might result in a new home run record. Of greater significance was that Yankees' fans embraced Mantle, an "original" Yankee and booed Roger Maris because they didn't want Maris to break the Yankees' record.

The media influenced the fans. Maris was not "Ruthian." They wrote that it would be a shame if he and not Mantle set a new record. Others thought that he was "unworthy "of the record. When Maris and not Mickey, broke the record, the Mantle cheers never stopped and the Maris boos never ended.

"That's when people started liking me," Mantle said. "After Roger beat me in the home-run race in 1961, I couldn't do no wrong. Everywhere I went I got standing ovations. All I had to do was walk out on the field. Hey, what the hell? It's a lot better than having them boo you. I became the underdog, they hated him and liked me."

The time was passing so quickly it seemed as if we had been talking only a couple of minutes. The flight attendant brought Mickey's scotch as he reclined in his seat and closed his eyes. I took it as a hint to leave. "Mickey, it was really great talking. This is something I'll always remember." Mickey was out like a light.

I returned to my seat. Mickey had told me that he was on his way to the New York Coliseum where he would appear at a sporting goods show. I hated to leave but little did I know that almost 20 years later, Mickey and I would be at the New York Coliseum promoting a video project we had worked on together.

As the plane touched down in New York, I used my considerable bulk to position myself next to Mickey as he walked off the ramp. What a scene it was. Here I was coming home from Texas, not Vietnam, and my family had seen me only a few months before, during the summer. So naturally there were literally 15, maybe 20 family members at the gate waiting to welcome me, which was not unusual for a first-born Italian son who graduated college and made his family "proud."

The first person that spotted me was my younger brother, Stephen, who was ten years old. "There's Tommy with Mickey Mantle!" Stephen was told to shut up in three Italian dialects and was viewed as having gone loony. But once everyone took their eyes off me, they spotted Mickey! *They* now became the first herd of deer in the headlights!

Mickey passed by my family and I made some silly attempt at introductions. We all stared as he waited for his transportation to arrive. What a fantastic feeling to introduce Mickey Mantle to my family. How great it was that Mickey Mantle, the man who hit the longest home runs in baseball history, made us feel so at ease, as if he were just another guy you might meet on a plane.

I often recalled the scene and finally, after Mickey passed away, I realized the incongruity of the situation. His loving family surrounded the individual who was ecstatic to meet his idol, a privilege that millions of others like him would have given almost anything to experience, while the idol waited alone for car service.

Once home, my father, uncle, grandfather and brothers all wanted to know the events leading up to my meeting with Mickey Mantle. I told them the highlights of how I recognized him and how Sgt. Major Kerr and General George S. Patton had helped me with my plan. My mom and grandmother had only a passing interest in this. They just wanted to know if I were hungry, and were worried that my 212-pound body looked thin!

CHAPTER 4

STALKING MICKEY AND ROGER

In the early 1970s, Mickey Mantle virtually disappeared from the sports pages and celebrity circles, although I would occasionally see him in a TV commercial or at World Series or All-Star games. He did some broadcasting and coaching for the Yankees, but it was short-lived and nothing replaced playing baseball for Mickey or for his fans.

We did have one great Mickey Mantle baseball experience left each year, however, thanks to the wonderful Yankees' tradition, started officially in 1946, of Old Timers' Day. It was always the highlight of my baseball year. During the 1950s and early 1960s, Mel Allen, the Voice of the Yankees, was the master of ceremonies. I remember how ancient the old timers seemed and how I didn't really identify with the cheers some of the less famous players received. It never crossed my mind that someday Mickey would be introduced as an old.

During the 1970s, Frank Messer was the lead Yankees' announcer. A no nonsense broadcaster who did a fine job describing the game, Messer handled the Old Timers' Days duties almost as well as Mel Allen. The former Baltimore Orioles' second banana to the great Chuck Thompson stood at a microphone behind home plate as he made the introductions. Each player's name was preceded by a little blurb that allowed fans to anticipate his identity. Mickey Mantle and Joe DiMaggio were always the last two introductions. Both always received thunderous ovations and I always thought back to the time when Mickey was an active player. Who didn't?

Joe DiMaggio deserved being introduced last. It was public knowledge that he would not attend Old Timers' Day if he were not the last player introduced and referred to as baseball's "Greatest Living Player." It was a ranking DiMaggio had received in 1969 when baseball, celebrating its 100th anniversary, awarded him the title. No one can stop the passage of time and by the mid-1980s, many of the Yankee Clipper's fans had passed away. Much to DiMaggio's displeasure, the fan's ovation to Mickey surpassed his own.

After the introductions, the invitees played a three-inning game. Mickey almost always participated, which made us feel that time had stood still or that we were back in the past, at least temporarily. I made these games must viewing for my future bride, Kathleen. She was very kind and even acted interested.

During the 1973 Old Timers' Day game, Mickey came to the plate, once again rekindling memories of how it used to be. Slowly and deliberately stepping into the batter's box, he took his right-handed batting stance, awaited the pitch and hit a long drive down the left field line. It barely went foul.

This small glimpse of what it was like in the 1950s and 1960s ignited the crowd into frenzy. The noise was deafening as Mickey, locked-in batting right-handed, drove the next pitch over the old Yankee Stadium 402-foot sign in left field.

"The Commerce Comet" literally limped around the bases and seemed to get as much of a kick out of the home run as did the crowd. I jumped out of my mezzanine seat and began yelling, "Yeah, yeah…the Mick!" I never thought I'd ever see another Mickey Mantle home run but I did. Kathleen had seen her first Mickey Mantle home run. I sat down and closed my eyes for a second. In my mind, in my imagination, in my memory, Mickey Mantle had never retired. Mickey never lost his power. Some old baseball players don't fade away and the truly great ones may lose their speed, but they never lose their pride.

In the early eighties, I developed a promotional campaign award, based upon the results of the preceding season, for "The Best Pinch-Hitter" in major league baseball. To publicize the award, my company took a table at the prestigious Baseball Writers' Association of America dinner. I was allowed to present the award at the podium. To my great delight, Mickey Mantle was also getting an award and would be on the dais. Mickey told me several years later that he got those awards simply because his presence sold tickets and generated publicity.

I somehow got up the nerve, as I had on the plane, to approach Mickey to mention our meeting seventeen years earlier. I must have been extremely optimistic to think he would remember me and I wasn't sure he did. Mickey was feeling no pain when I told him that he was the real "Natural," which brings us back to the "what-ifs."

Baseball was hot that year. The movie *The Natural* was receiving a lot of publicity. Mickey was often compared to Robert Redford's character. Bernard Malamud created Roy Hobbs, who could have been "the best there ever was" if a romantic encounter hadn't nearly cost him his life and if he weren't extremely attracted to females. As my friendship with Mickey developed over the next few years, it was obvious that Mickey, like Roy Hobbs, was a great baseball player who enjoyed being with women.

National Geographic had interviewed *The Natural's* producer, Barry Levinson, for the book, *Baseball as America*. Levinson stated, "There's a measure of regret in the careers of many ballplayers. Mickey Mantle, at the end, spoke of regret he had about never living up to his potential. Baseball players are endowed with a certain kind of extraordinary talent. Some ultimately abuse that talent, or are injured and then their youth is gone. But there's a brief, precious window of time when an athlete has such remarkable physical ability, after which the talent can't be brought back. It can be a very dramatic story."

Mickey's behavior on the dais that night was shocking and disappointing. After a few introductory remarks, he began a verbal barrage against former Yankees' General Manager George Weiss. Mickey and Weiss had had a contentious relationship because they were involved in several bitter contract negotiations. In fact, Weiss wanted to cut Mantle's salary after the 1957 season when Mickey hit a career high .365, with an on base percentage of .512! He was the American League's Most Valuable Player for the second consecutive season, but Weiss reasoned that Mickey hadn't won the Triple Crown as he had in 1956, so he deserved a salary cut.

Lonesome George, as he was referred to privately by some writers because money was his only friend, even threatened to trade Mickey to the Cleveland Indians for Rocky Colavito. Only the intervention of Yankees' owners Dan Topping and Del Webb prevented a seismic shift in baseball history. Mickey alluded to how he almost became a Cleveland Indian because of the "cheap bastard George Weiss." He continued with a barrage of X-rated, liquor-fueled anecdotes before he calmed down and left the dais.

I was upset at Mickey's behavior although I empathized with him since he had made some excellent points. A player who had Mickey's 1957 season shouldn't have to fight a cut in pay, yet despite understanding Mickey's long held hard feelings toward George Weiss, I felt that his behavior was outrageously inappropriate. There were women and a few children present who were stunned and embarrassed. Mickey got "a pass" on his bad behavior because he was Mickey Mantle. Only Greer stood up to him.

If a modern celebrity acted the way Mickey did, the incident would be splashed all over the newspapers, television screens and Internet. In 1984, Mickey's actions were downplayed. Remember, he spoke before the Baseball Writers' Association of America's dinner. The room was filled with reporters who were always looking to scoop each other, but Mickey had earned or at least had obtained their silence.

I went over some of the things that Mickey had said. I never knew that Mickey had almost been traded to the Indians. I knew how I, a 13-year old Tom Molito, would have felt if Mickey had become a Cleveland Indian. I almost hate to admit it, but speaking for the kid I used to be, I would have become an Indians' fan and would have always resented the Yankees' management. It was for good reason that when George Weiss finally retired, the joke that circulated among the baseball writers was that Mrs. Weiss complained, "I married George for better or for worse…but not for lunch."

As Mickey moved away from the dais, I thought of how ironic it was that in 1968, he and Rocky Colavito became Yankees teammates. The 1968 Yankees finished fifth in the 10-team American League, but what is most amazing to me is that the Yankees won 83 games with a .214 batting average. It was the lowest team batting average in Yankees' history. Nineteen-sixty-eight was the "year of the pitcher," which is a euphemism for the fact that the balance between pitching and hitting no longer existed. The pitchers were getting bigger and stronger due to better nutrition and training and so were the hitters, but hitting depends on reflexes. It is difficult for hitters to improve their reaction time. Following the 1968 season, the pitching mound was lowered from a height of 15 inches to 10 inches in an attempt to restore the balance.

Mickey had his worst season in 1968, hitting only .237 with 18 home runs and an anemic .398 slugging average. He often lamented that his greatest regret was losing his .300 lifetime batting average.

In an attempt to help a challenged offense, on July 15, 1968, the eighth-place Yankees (they weren't last because there were 10 teams in the league) signed Rocky Colavito, who had been released by the Los Angeles Dodgers. The new Bronx bomber fit in well, considering the circumstances. Rocky, who batted only .220, had one memorable game that was the highlight of the Yankees' season.

The Yankees were playing a Sunday doubleheader on August 25 against the Detroit Tigers, after having just played the Tigers a doubleheader on Friday, in which the second game ended as a 3-3 tie after 19 innings. Unlike today, teams played regularly scheduled doubleheaders until the baseball moguls realized that two admissions are more profitable than one.

Those Sundays of my past were glorious baseball marathons. A 2 P.M. sun-drenched Yankee Stadium would become a 5 P.M. field of shadows, only to be transformed into baseball battlefield that needed artificial lights to avoid being in almost total darkness.

By the top of the fourth inning of the first game, the Yankees trailed the Tigers, 5-0, with Tigers' runners on first and second and one out. Yankees' skipper Ralph Houk didn't have much left in his bullpen so he summoned Rocky Colavito into the game to pitch. The crowd was delighted. Rocky had one of the best arms of any outfielder who ever played. The problem was his arm was almost as erratic as it was powerful. He always joked that he would make a pretty good pitcher. On this day, Colavito confidently strode in from the right field bullpen, took his warm up pitches and retired Al Kaline and Willie Horton, stranding the runners to keep the deficit at 5-0.

The Yankees rallied and with Colavito still pitching, scored five times in the sixth inning to take a 7-6 lead. Houk didn't want to press his luck so he quickly yanked Colavito. The overworked bullpen protected the one run margin as Rocco got the victory, which was his first and only major league pitching win.

Rocky Colavito came up with the Indians briefly in 1955. He became a regular in 1956. The Indians traded him to the Tigers at the start of the 1960 season in a stunning deal that would never be made today. Colavito, the 1959 American League home run champ who hit 42 round trippers, was traded for Harvey Kuenn, the 1959 American League batting champ who hit .353. There were many debates. Is the home run champion or the batting champion more valuable? Well, Mickey once said, "If I went for singles the way Pete Rose does, I'd wear a dress."

I encountered Mickey again in 1985. My company had taken a table at the annual Yankees' Welcome Home Dinner, an event that occurs in a New York Hotel after spring training and just prior to the start of the baseball season. Our table included some of my business associates with their spouses or girlfriends.

There was a cocktail party that occupied several large rooms. As two of my friends from work and I turned a corner, much to my delight, we came upon Mickey Mantle. He was standing and with Yogi Berra and Roger Maris. The three of us just stopped and gawked at the three players. The fact that I had met Mickey before didn't matter, nor did the fact that seeing three Yankees greats at the Yankees' Welcome Home dinner should not have been considered unusual, but for baseball fans, particularly Catholic Yankees fans, meeting Mickey, Roger and Yogi was almost like meeting the Holy Trinity.

I spotted a photographer and commandeered his time. After handing him a $100 bill, I told him to take as many pictures of us with Mickey as possible. The result of this photo opportunity is now referred to as the "stalker sessions." In some shots, my head appears just over Mickey's shoulder, while in others I am with Yogi, or Roger, or with all three. Mickey looked me straight in the eye and with his boyish grin, pointed to me as he told Roger and Yogi, "I know this guy from someplace." Yogi was Yogi, but what pleased me was that Roger was even more accommodating than Mickey. He posed for picture after picture and even got Yogi to put a big cigar in his mouth.

The dinner was on April 15, the night of the legendary Hagler-Hearns fight. Our group wandered off after the dinner and found ourselves at Jimmy Wesson's bar, a famous sports hangout. There was a TV in the bar that was tuned to the fight. I ordered a Rusty Nail. Since I don't drink much, that would probably be the only drink that I would order. Then I noticed that there was a broad shoulder in front of me. It was Mickey! I glanced to my left, made eye contact, and smiled at Roger Maris. Talk about serendipity. We were at the right place at the right time and we knew it. They tell me it was one of the greatest fights of all time. I saw it with one eye. The other eye watched Mickey and Roger.

Mickey, of course, had his usual allotment of alcohol. Roger just watched the fight, seemingly a little ill at ease. Mickey was having a great time. Looking at him, it would be hard to believe that he once was more uncomfortable than Roger in such environments. Except for me, the crowd was interested in the fight, not in Roger, who never got used to the New York scene. He was more a of a country boy than Mickey that wouldn't or couldn't adjust – probably the former.

I saw the human side of these rural-bred men, Mickey from Oklahoma and Roger from North Dakota. What a stark contrast existed. Mickey was in his adopted, now-natural element. He had been frequenting New York City nightspots for well over a quarter of a century. His movements were natural; his expressions were confident. He was at ease. Roger, on the other hand, gave me the feeling that he was someplace not of his choosing; that he would rather be someplace else. He seemed stiff and uncomfortable, having a polite drink with an old friend. He also didn't look well. Unfortunately, his untimely death was in the near future.

Mickey Mantle and Roger Maris hit a still-standing season record of 115 home runs for two teammates in 1961. Roger broke Babe Ruth's record of 60 home runs and still (2015) holds the single-season American League mark. Mickey hit 54 that season before being forced to the sidelines by the flu and his hip injury.

Many experts think Roger broke the record for one compelling reason. In 80 percent of his at-bats, Mickey hit fourth, behind Roger. Maris did not receive even *one* intentional walk the entire season. With Mickey batting behind him, Roger batted .293. When Mickey was not in the lineup, Roger hit an anemic .174. The difference in Maris' home run frequency was astounding. When Mickey batted after him, Roger averaged one home run every 8.8 at-bats. Without Mickey's looming presence, Roger managed one home run every 16.4 at-bats.

A friend of mine started watching Mickey in 1951. His son, who, like millions of his generation, wishes he had seen Mickey play, met Ralph Houk in 2001 at an autograph show. "Doc" asked Houk why he batted Roger ahead of Mickey. Houk politely replied that he had been asked the question thousands of times, he had his reasons and it would take much too long to explain it again.

My belief is that if Roger batted behind Mickey, they still wouldn't give Mickey many good pitches to hit, even if it meant putting Mickey on for Roger. No offense meant, but neither Bill Skowron, Elston Howard, nor an aging Yogi was a Mickey Mantle. Well, Yogi was fearsome, especially when it counted the most. It is possible that if Roger followed Mickey in the line up, neither would have broken the record.

Bobby Richardson usually led off for the Yankees, followed by Tony Kubek and then Roger Maris. If they were retired in order, Mickey would lead off the next inning with the bases empty. Unless he hit a home run, he would not drive home a run. Of course, Mickey walked much more than Roger, so Mickey leading off an inning often gave the Yankees a runner on first with no outs, bringing up either Bill "Moose" Skowron, Yogi Berra, or Elston Howard. Houk did have that important point in his favor. Despite that, there was another side to the coin.

When Mickey batted third, as he had under Casey Stengel, a Mantle walk in the first inning would bring the Yankees' clean-up hitter to the plate with at least one runner on base. To this day, I am convinced Maris broke the record because of Mickey's ominous presence. I was devastated and deeply disappointed by Mickey's late season injury that stalled his home run total at a prodigious, "pre-steroid era" 54.

During Mickey and Roger's playing days, the press attempted to portray a jealousy or animosity between them. The newspapers revived and wrote about the friction between Babe Ruth and Lou Gehrig, which was real, in an attempt to connect their relationship with the one between Mickey and Roger. The fact is that nothing could have been further from the truth.

Mickey and Roger liked and respected each other. *The Sporting News* reveals that the home run record chase didn't move them farther apart. It brought them closer together. Mantle sincerely appreciated what Roger added to the Yankees lineup while Roger, like everyone else, was close to being awed by Mickey's power and speed. "What was born was a deep friendship, rooted by the similarities of their backgrounds and the intense spotlight they were destined to share."

An intensely revealing comment made in 1961 epitomizes Mickey Mantle. When asked about the chase for the home run record and Roger Maris, Mickey was supportive of Roger. Pressed about how he would feel if Roger, not he, broke the record, Mickey simply stated it made no difference because Roger was a Yankee and then followed with, "I'll always be a Yankee." In the end, it wouldn't matter whether Mickey or Roger set a new record. Babe Ruth, Mickey Mantle, and Roger Maris were all Yankees.

During the 1961 season, Roger, Mickey and Bob Cerv shared an unpretentious apartment in Queens. Roger would often make breakfast. On afternoons before night games, the three would putt golf balls into a little tin hole on top of the carpet, betting pennies on the outcome. After all, these were the days before free agency, so pennies counted. Later, Roger usually drove the three of them to the ballpark in his convertible. At Maris' funeral, a very distraught Mantle was overheard to comment several times that Roger might not have been the best ball player, but he'd never met a better man.

More than a decade after attending the early 1980s Baseball Writers' Association of America dinner, I was at a 1995 event, where a sober Mickey appeared with Willie Mays and Duke Snider. Mickey started his speech by saying, "They tell me I was at this dinner once before…but I don't remember!" And then he apologized and warned the kids in the audience of his old fast lifestyle and how it had not served him well. Little did we know that it was his last public appearance in New York.

CHAPTER 5

BREAKFAST OF CHAMPIONS

It was 1988 and one thing was certain. I was now traveling in New York City's high priced neighborhoods. After the initial meeting with Mickey and Greer on Park Avenue, we started to assemble the production "team" for the *500 Home Run Club* video at Mickey's restaurant on Central Park West. Mickey had opened the restaurant in the mid-1980s after being approached by several investors. It quickly became *the* sports bar in New York City, reminding many of both Toots Shor's and Jack Dempsey's legendary hangouts. Mickey used to live at the Saint Moritz Hotel next door to the restaurant, which made it easy for him to frequent the hotel's bar. Mickey had little to do with running Mickey Mantle's restaurant. All he had to do was lend his name and make one monthly appearance. He fulfilled his yearly requirement the first month!

The restaurant was a Mantle fan's dream. The walls were covered with hundreds of photographs and paintings of Mickey, many of which were magazine covers of Mickey with other famous people. There was baseball memorabilia, including bats, balls and player uniforms. The food had a southern accent. Chicken fried steak was the house specialty of the basically traditional American menu. Mickey had lowered the prices when the restaurant opened to make it more affordable to working class families. I'm sure the move stemmed from his family values that developed when he was a boy in Dust Bowl Oklahoma during the 1930s. The wait staff all wore the number seven on their baseball uniform shirts. They were attractive and seemed to enjoy the environment. The girls even seemed to enjoy Mickey's flirting.

Our morning meeting was held in the back of the restaurant beneath a giant mural of the old Yankee Stadium, with Mickey batting on a beautiful sun-lit day. The mural was magnificent and gave me the feeling that I was in the stands at the Stadium with Mickey at the plate, about to make contact. I felt joy and sadness. Joy because I had the privilege of seeing Mickey play and sadness because it was from a time lost forever. A waitress brought Mickey what he laughingly called "The Breakfast of Champions," which was a combination of Kalhua, orange juice and vodka.

When Mickey asked me if I wanted to join him, I politely declined. As I look back, there was never a time that Mickey and I were together that alcohol wasn't present. Experts are divided with respect to the role genetics plays in alcoholism, but Mickey, Mickey Jr., David and Danny were all treated for the addiction.

Mickey was extremely well liked by his teammates and most of his opponents. During the 1950s, a World Series share, especially a winning share, made a significant difference, sometimes equaling a player's yearly salary. It is common knowledge that Hank Bauer, who was close to Mickey, would discipline teammates, especially rookies or new teammates, if they didn't hustle. When it came to Mickey, playing hard was never a problem. Being in shape for a game could be.

Bauer tells the story of how he confronted Mickey when Mickey walked into the locker room almost completely stoned. Bauer tried to talk to Mickey about it, but before Hank could get started, Mickey told him that he was going to die of Hodgkin's disease before he reached 40. He didn't want to get cheated out of life because he would have a short one. Hank patted Mickey on the shoulder and walked away.

Mickey looked at the glass he was holding as a broad smile ran across his face. He just stared at me as if he were waiting for me to ask what was so amusing. So I did. Mickey asked me if I knew what Whitey Ford had told sportswriter Phil Pepe, who covered the New York Yankees from 1961-84.

"Mickey, Pepe has written a lot about Whitey. What are you smiling about?"

Mickey related that Ford had given Pepe an interview in which he told the writer that he doesn't object to pitchers doctoring the baseball. Ford also said that if it meant he had to cheat in order to keep throwing his good stuff, he would do it, in part because of the money. If salaries had been as high in the 1960s as in the late 1980s, Mickey said that Ford told Pepe he would have tried to pitch into his 40s. He would have used whatever help he needed to get out the hitters.

"You know," Mickey said, grinning even more than before, "Whitey used to put mud and dirt on the ball. He put saliva to one side of the ball and then rubbed it into the dirt as he reached for the rosin bag. That's why we called him 'Slick.'"

The meeting itself dissected the mechanics of the video shoot, which would consist of Bob Costas discussing the various 500 Home Run Club players with Mickey, historic film clips and many photographs and statistics woven in. I was really confident that the video would be successful. Mickey, Bob Costas and Bob Sheppard, the Yankee Stadium public address announcer who would introduce each of the 500 Home Run Club members, were professionals, fans loved home run hitters and there was an excellent mixture of players from different eras.

During the meeting, I again saw a side of Mickey that could be crude and awkward. Someone at the meeting off-handedly asked Greer Johnson what her job was working with Mickey. Before she could answer, Mickey, in an attempt at humor, replied, "She fluffs my pillow!" Greer was far from nonplussed. "Maybe so Mick, but not tonight!" Everyone from the *Cabin Fever Entertainment* production team laughed uncomfortably and I admired her poised response.

Mickey had given Greer a cheap shot that undermined her credibility as a businesswoman who wanted to be taken seriously among a group of men. I really liked Greer and thought my hero had acted like a jerk. Women had adored Mickey Mantle since he arrived in 1951 and he knew it. He often took women for granted and used them for brief encounters.

When the meeting broke up, I said goodbye to Mickey and started walking away. "Don't you want my autograph?" Mickey asked. "Oh, okay," I replied. Mickey took out one of the cards he carried, designed by Greer, and signed his name. It had his picture and some statistical information. It illustrated how Greer helped Mickey deal with his enormous celebrity.

In the book, *The Last Hero: The Life of Mickey Mantle* by David Faulkner, Greer explains, "We started taking cards with us that we pre-signed whenever we went to airports. For people to come up to you that way it sometimes takes a lot of courage and they must love you absolutely to death to do it. So for you then to turn around and be ugly to them, that's the only time they're probably ever going to meet you in person, and you're their hero, and that's what they are going to remember about you."

When Mickey lashed out at someone, according to Greer, he always knew that if he knowingly hurt someone's feelings he'd think about it for days afterwards. He could crush people and he just didn't realize it.

I put the card in my briefcase and looked at it when I got home. "Dear Tom, F.... you! Mick."

Crude? Yes, but it's one of my most cherished possessions. My daughter Laura has requested that she get the framed card when I go to the "great Ball Park in the sky." Mickey's inscription was a sign that he liked me enough to joke with me. I'm not sure Greer reacted the same way when they returned to the Regency.

CHAPTER 6

THE "500 HOME RUN CLUB"

Mickey arrived the day of the video shoot in a foul mood. Everyone was assembled in the hallowed Yankees' locker room, the inner sanctum of Ruth, Gehrig, DiMaggio, Berra, Maris, Ford and Mantle. Mickey had entered this room for the first time in 1951, a scared 19-year-old, afraid to even glance at Joe DiMaggio, much less speak to him. Over the years, in this room, an ecstatic Mickey Mantle had celebrated many great moments. It was in this room that a disconsolate Mickey Mantle would have to accept some crushing disappointments.

Mickey's spirits suddenly did an about face when he saw Bob Costas. Greer's appearance with Mickey's "Breakfast of Champions added to the positive mood." Mickey sat at his old locker next to Costas, with all the uniforms of the 500 Club members surrounding them in the background, hanging backwards to expose their numbers:

3 Babe Ruth
3 Harmon Killebrew
4 Mel Ott
7 Mickey Mantle
9 Ted Williams
#14 Ernie Banks
#20 Frank Robinson
#20 Mike Schmidt
#24 Willie Mays
#30 Jimmy Foxx
#41 Eddie Mathews

#44 Hank Aaron
#44 Willie McCovey
#44 Reggie Jackson
#1 Japan's Sadaharu Oh

Another of Mickey's favorites, Yankee Stadium public address announcer Bob Sheppard, would be the voice on the video who would introduced each 500 Club member's segment. Bob Sheppard had taken the job at Yankee Stadium in April 1951. The first game he announced was the Yankees' home opener against the Boston Red Sox. The first player he ever introduced was a DiMaggio—Joe's brother Dom.

After Bob Sheppard introduced Dom, the little center fielder led off the game with a ringing single off Yankees' starter Vic Raschi. Billy Goodman followed with a blooper into short center field that appeared to be another single, but Joe DiMaggio made a spectacular shoestring catch off his shoe tops and fired a strike to first base to double up his brother Dom. Raschi went on to shutout Boston, as the Yankees coasted to a 5-0 victory. Mickey got his first major league hit in Bob Sheppard's first game, and Whitey Ford, who was in the army, threw out the ceremonial first pitch.

When asked recently which names he enjoyed announcing the most, Bob Sheppard replied, "Of all the names I have announced, my favorite is Mickey Mantle. My other favorites are Alvaro Espinosa, Jose Valdivielso, Salome Barojas, and Shigetoshi Hasegawa. Mickey Mantle is the perfect name because the two 'Ms' make it alliterative and the 'L' sounds very good.

"Shortly before he died," Sheppard continued, "we were both being interviewed on a television program. All of a sudden, he turned to me and said -- on the air -- that every time he heard me announce his name, he got goose bumps. And I felt the same way about announcing him."

Bob Sheppard had announced for the football Giants almost as long as he had for the Yankees. His voice is so dignified that it led Reggie Jackson to remark that, "Bob Sheppard's words sound like the Voice of God."

Dignity does not necessarily exclude humor. Sheppard was working the NFL Championship Game between the Baltimore Colts and New York Giants at Yankee Stadium on December 28, 1958. The game is considered one of the great classics in the history of football, one that has become an integral part of the lore and legend of not only the NFL, but also of Yankee Stadium.

In a hard fought battle between two great teams, the Giants appeared to have the championship won late in the fourth quarter, or at least that is what Bob Sheppard thought. "I can remember thinking late in the game that the Giants had won it and they punted down toward the home plate area of the field to the 20-yard line. Unitas had to go 80 yards and the Giants were a good defensive team. But he started a great drive and I kept announcing 'Unitas to Berry,' 'Unitas to Berry,' 'Unitas to Berry.' I wanted to scream into my microphone, 'Would somebody cover Berry.' I felt I was stuttering 'Unitas to Berry.'"

We had shot an opening scene for the video before Mickey arrived. When I entered the Yankees' locker room, I never, in my wildest dreams as a kid or as a businessman, thought that this day would ever occur. I put my notepad on the locker shelf that belonged to Mickey Mantle. For an instant, I was in a Yankees uniform, about to leave the locker room for the runway to face Jim Bunning or Frank Lary.

My eight-year-old son Luke brought me back to reality when he asked me, "Who was Jimmy Foxx?" I had brought Luke along and, just like a typical little leaguer; he was looking up at all the uniforms. The irony of Luke asking about Jimmy Foxx crossed my mind, since alcohol was as much an enemy to Foxx as it was to Mickey. I said to Luke, half-jokingly that "Jimmy Foxx is the guy who hit all those long home runs that Mickey's home run beat." Luke just looked at me quizzically, the way kids do.

I introduced Luke to Mickey, who wanted to know what position Luke played. What a great moment it was. What a great moment it would be for any parent. My son was talking to Mickey. Fathers want only the best for their kids and thanks to good fortune and some initiative on my part, Luke had an experience he would never forget. Neither would I.

Luke disappeared and it didn't take a psychic to figure out where he went. A few minutes later, a Yankees security guard came in and told us to "get the kid off the field!" Luke was having a grand time running and sliding in an empty Yankee Stadium, imitating his idol, Rickey Henderson, who was another great example of awesome speed and power.

The *500 Home Run Club* video opened with Babe Ruth. The three of us, Bob Costas, Mickey Mantle, and Tom Molito, talked baseball as we "worked." Costas, who was great to work with, told Mickey that Ruth hit homers so high that he was responsible for ball parks installing foul poles, since no one had ever hit balls that high and far! Mickey wasn't surprised since so many of his home runs were "Ruthian blasts." I told Costas that I thought ballparks always had foul poles.

Just as Jimmy Foxx and Mickey had alcohol as a problem, Babe and Mickey both had great appetites for women. Harvey Frommer, in *Five O'Clock Lightning*, related that Babe was a regular at "houses of ill repute," whose professionals referred to themselves as "sporting girls."

Ted Williams followed Babe Ruth in the video. Costas mentioned that there is a great story about the extremely confident Williams, who always wanted to be remembered as the greatest hitter of all time. When he was a rookie, someone told Williams, "Wait until you see Jimmy Foxx hit." Foxx finished his career with 534 home runs, which had been second only to Ruth's 714 for many years. What was Williams' reply? "Wait till Foxx sees me hit!"

During the Williams segment, Mickey spoke about the time he sat in the American League dugout before an All-Star game discussing hitting techniques with the perfectionist, Ted Williams. Mickey said, "Ted got me so confused that I didn't get a hit for two weeks!"

In his book, *The Science of Hitting*, Williams states that one thing was 95 percent certain -- he was going to take the first pitch the first time he batted in a game. Williams was a firm believer in being selective at the plate and not helping the pitcher out by being anxious. So was Mickey, at least most of the time, although Mickey did say that Williams was a scientific hitter who hated to strike out, while he "went for the fences with almost every swing."

In the video, Costas pointed out that eight of the 14 hitters with 500 home runs had entered the major leagues in the 1950s. Mickey's great sense of humor kicked in. "They must have had some bad pitching in those days!"

Mickey, Willie Mays, Eddie Mathews, Henry Aaron, Ernie Banks, Frank Robinson, Harmon Killebrew and Willie McCovey all broke into the majors during the 1950s, but Mickey really was kidding around about the pitching. There were some great pitchers, including Jim Bunning, Don Drysdale, Bob Feller, Whitey Ford, Bob Lemon, Robin Roberts, Warren Spahn, Hoyt Wilhelm and Early Wynn, all of whom are Hall of Famers. Among the 500 Home Run Club members, Mickey played on the most World Championship teams (seven), but Ted Williams, Willie McCovey, Harmon Killebrew, and Ernie Banks never were on a World Championship team. Great players need a strong supporting cast.

Younger fans have been accustomed to teams, especially American

League teams with a designated hitter, having three or four batters with 20 or more home runs, but when Mickey won the Triple Crown in 1956, he hit 52, Vic Wertz finished second with 32 and Yogi hit 30. No other American League hitter managed to hit as many as 30 home runs.

In 1947, the Baseball Writers' Association of America initiated the Rookie of the Year award. The award winners among the fourteen 500 Home Run Club Members are Willie Mays (1951 NL), Frank Robinson (1956 NL), and Willie McCovey (1959 NL). If there had been a Rookie of the Year award prior to 1947, it is likely that Babe Ruth would have won it in 1915, but not as a slugger. In 1915, left-handed Boston Red Sox pitcher Babe Ruth won 18 games, lost only eight, and had a 2.44 ERA. In his first season primarily as an everyday player, Babe hit 29 home runs to set a new single season record.

Mickey and Willie Mays, like Ted Williams, reached the major leagues while basically youngsters, but Mel Ott, who led the National League in career home runs, RBIs, runs scored and walks when he retired in 1947, began playing for the New York Giants when he was 17. Ott was only five-feet nine-inches tall. He weighed about 170 pounds. His home field was the Polo Grounds, where it was allegedly 257 feet down the right field line at ground level and an even more inviting 248 feet from home at the second deck overhang. The left-handed hitter learned to pull the ball sharply to take advantage of the park. In 1930, it was 505 feet to straight away center field, a distance that changed throughout the baseball seasons, but which was always close to 480 feet. Don't hit straightway was Ott's motto.

Mickey and Frank Robinson were Triple Crown winners, Mickey in 1956 and Robinson 10 years later. Their great seasons were remarkably similar (.353, 52, 130 for Mickey and .316, 49, 122 for Frank), although Mickey's batting average was considerably higher. Frank was one of baseball's great all-around players, not only one of the game's great home run hitters. He belongs in the same class with Mickey, Willie Mays, Henry Aaron, Roberto Clemente, and of course, Jackie Robinson, who never had the chance to join the 500 Home Run Club.

Mickey faced Willie Mays' Giants in the 1962 World Series, the only time their teams ever faced each other in meaningful games since Mickey and Willie's rookie year, but Mickey didn't play a role in the final drama of the 1962 Series. It was Willie Mays, Willie McCovey and Roger Maris. Mickey recalled the seventh game of that Series, as Bob Costas and I listened. Of course, we both knew what happened.

In the ninth inning, Willie Mays came to the plate with two outs and the speedy Matty Alou on first, representing the potential tying run in a 1-0 game. Willie wasted no time hitting a hard drive down the right field line for an extra base hit. The ball rolled near the right field line as Alou raced to third. Everyone thought that he would score the tying run, but everyone underrated the Yankees' right fielder. Roger Maris made one of the great plays in World Series history by cutting off the ball before it could roll to the fence, forcing Alou to stop at third. Willie McCovey was the batter.

Mickey told us that he remembered thinking that the Yankees should intentionally walk McCovey to face the lesser of two evils, Orlando Cepeda because Cepeda batted from the right side of the plate. He modestly said he really was hoping that the ball would be hit to him.

Yankees' skipper Ralph Houk asked Yankees' starting pitcher Ralph Terry if he would rather face the right-handed hitting Orlando Cepeda instead of McCovey. There was no thought of taking Terry out of the game. In 1962, starters were supposed to finish what they started.

Terry told Houk he could get McCovey. Yes, Terry retired McCovey -- on one of the hardest hit balls anyone had ever seen, but fortunately for the Yankees and Terry, McCovey's line drive didn't kill second baseman Bobby Richardson, who hung on to end the World Series.

Mickey was truly a humble man. Even as a player he did nothing to bring attention to himself. When Costas and Mickey were discussing Mickey's 536 lifetime homers, Mickey told him that he walked 1,800 times and struck out 1,700 during his 18-year career. "This means, based on 500 at bats a year, I went seven years without hitting the ball!"

As we worked on the video, my thoughts bounced from the present to my memories of Mickey's career. Even though he told Bob Costas that he had gone the equivalent of seven years without hitting the ball, I remember when Mickey did hit the ball. And did he hit it. Like no other hitter ever hit it.

My first memory is Memorial Day 1956. I'm at my local ball field, Welty Field in Yonkers, N.Y. There was a sudden commotion and I heard "Mickey hit the roof." No one had ever hit a ball out of Yankee Stadium. No one ever will. Mickey's ball came within 18 inches of bouncing onto the Bronx pavement. In the June 18, 1956 issue of *Sports Illustrated*, Robert Creamer eloquently described the event.

"A thick bodied, pleasant faced young man, carrying a bat, stood at home plate in Yankee Stadium, turned the blond bullet head on his bull's neck toward Pedro Ramos, a pitcher employed by the Washington Senators, watched intently the flight of the baseball thrown toward him, bent his knees, dropped his right shoulder slightly toward the ball, clenched his bat and raised it to a near perfect perpendicular."

Twisting his massive torso under the guidance of a magnificently tuned set of reflexes, Mickey Mantle so controlled the exorbitant strength generated by his legs, back, shoulders and arms that he brought through the plane of the flight of the pitch with a precision which propelled the ball immensely high and far toward the right field roof, so high and far that old timers in the crowd, thinking perhaps of Babe Ruth, watched in awe and held their breath.

For no one had ever hit a fair ball over the majestic height of the gray green façade that looms above the three tiers of grandstand seats, in this, the greatest of ballparks. Indeed, in the thirty-three years since the Stadium was opened, not one of the great company of home run hitters who have batted there, including Babe Ruth, Lou Gehrig, Joe DiMaggio, Jimmy Foxx, Hank Greenberg and just about everyone else you can think of, had even come close to hitting a fair ball over the giant sized filigree hanging from the lip of the stands which, in both left and right field, hooks far into fair territory toward the bleachers.

Mantle hit the filigree. He came so close to making history that he made it. The ball struck high on the facade, barely a foot or two below the edge of the roof. Ever since, as people come into the stadium and find their seats, almost invariably their eyes wander to THE SPOT. Arms point and people stare in admiration. Then they turn to the field and seek out Mantle.

Mickey Mantle hit home runs that reached the façade in right field at Yankee Stadium more than once. Most fans don't know that the first time a Mickey Mantle home run hit the façade was on May 5, 1956 against Kansas City's Ed Burtschy. The ball hit the façade near the foul line but didn't generate the excitement the one he hit a few weeks later off Ramos created because it was so close to the foul pole, only 296 feet from home plate.

Seven years later, on May 22, 1963, Mickey hit a delivery off Bill Fischer of the Kansas City A's against the façade with the ball still in its upward flight to give the Yankees an 11 inning win. Famed biologist Stephen Jay Gould attended that game and years later described the event in the

December, 1986 issue of *Sport Magazine*:

"I took a trip to New York a month before my graduation from college in 1963. On May 22, Mantle batting lefty, hit a line drive off Kansas City pitcher Bill Fischer. It rose and rose until it struck the façade above the third deck in right field - the closest that anyone had ever come to hitting a fair ball out of Yankee Stadium ("the hardest ball I ever hit," Mantle told me.) It was still actually rising when it struck the parapet. I remember particularly the stunned silence before the roar of the crowd. Six more feet up and Mantle would have fused himself to my profession of scientific exploration in more than the abstract character of excellence. Six more feet up and that ball would have become a moon of Uranus."

Costas, Mickey and I were so absorbed in discussing baseball that we hardly noticed it was time for a lunch break. There was a large table a short distance from Mickey's old locker. We eagerly left our seats near Mickey's old locker and helped ourselves to a nice meal. Eating doesn't stop dyed-in-the-wool fans from talking baseball. Neither Costas, Mantle nor I ever tired of rehashing 1956. Our conversations continued.

Mickey had some great seasons, but 1956 was the magical year. No one can predict the future, but prior to the start of the season, *The Sporting News*, baseball's Bible, predicted that 1956 would be Mickey's break out year and that he would win the Triple Crown. It would be the season that he would become Mickey Mantle. When fans spoke about Mickey, the daunting phrase, "If he reaches his potential" was heard less and less frequently as the home runs were hit more and more frequently. By the middle of the season, there was an almost universal consensus that Mickey was the best player in the game. By the end of the season, that conclusion had been confirmed.

From the beginning, the season's pattern was set. Mickey hit two prodigious home runs against Washington's Camilio Pascual in spacious Griffith Stadium on opening day and took off from there. His batting average didn't fall below .400 until June 10. On June 21 against Tigers' lefty Billy Hoeft, Mickey hit home run numbers 27 and 28 to fuel speculation of surpassing Babe Ruth's single season record of 60.

Mickey Mantle captivated the entire nation. It was at about that time that the baseball writers pointed out how attitudes toward Mickey had changed. Unlike his first five seasons, the vociferous cheers easily drowned out the few boos. It wasn't just in the Bronx, and it wasn't just for Mickey Mantle that fans rooted. The Yankees drew huge crowds on the road and the home fans, sometimes grudgingly, recognized they were seeing excellence when they watched the 1956 Yankees and Mickey Mantle.

They said that Mickey Mantle "arrived" in 1956 when he won the Triple Crown, but the truth is that he really "arrived" when his contemporaries praised his achievements rather than his potential. Mantle at his peak barely approached Ted Williams as a hitter, but Williams knew how good Mantle had become. When asked if Mantle had a chance to bat .400, Williams didn't hesitate.

"Absolutely. Mickey has everything going for him. He has the speed to beat out bunts, so they can't play him too deep, and the power to drive it past them if they creep in on him. He hits both ways so you can't play him in any particular field," he said.

Casey Stengel agreed. "Williams is right," Stengel told reporters. "This boy has the chance to be a .400 hitter, especially when he has fellas behind him which will help him."

Joe DiMaggio, who was the MVP the year Williams hit .406, concurred. "Mickey has grown up," observed DiMaggio. "It takes some players longer to arrive than others. He has learned to pick out the ball he wants to hit. His real test will come when he goes 0-for-4 a couple games in a row."

Bill Dickey, one of the greatest of all catchers and a teammate of DiMaggio, was as impressed with Mantle as the others. "Mickey has strong wrists, powerful forearms and a back that a heavyweight champion wouldn't be ashamed of," Dickey told baseball writer Tom Meany.

Many fans that never saw Mantle play wonder why he didn't steal more bases, since he was one of the fastest runners in baseball history. Stengel explained it quite easily. "With all his speed, you would think now he would steal more bases, wouldn't you? There isn't any sense in stealing when you have fellas which can hit the ball out of the park," Stengel said. "You don't have to steal with Mantle, because you've seen him go from first to third, and from first to home too, as far as that's concerned, which he does faster than anybody playing ball today."

Stengel continued, explaining how amazing it was that Mantle was so great despite his bad legs. "Thing too many people overlook about him," said Stengel, "is that he's been doing all that he has been doing this year as a cripple. He still hasta have his right leg bandaged before every game. And that knee he had operated on a few years ago, after he fell over like he was dead in the World Series, still bothers him."

Mantle had a mediocre rookie season in 1951, but to show how much was expected from him, one can examine his 1952-55 seasons. He batted .303/. 408/. 542, averaging 32 home runs and 110 RBIs over a 162 - game season. He led the league with 37 home runs in 1955 and in runs scored in 1954, but he didn't become "Mickey Mantle" until 1956.

But not everyone in baseball rooted for Mickey. On the night of June 5 at Yankee Stadium, Kansas City Athletics manager Lou Boudreau, who had created the Ted Williams shift when he managed the Indians in 1946 by putting most of his fielders on the right side of the field in an attempt to thwart the left-handed hitting Williams, created the "Mantle shift."

Boudreau moved second baseman Jim Finigan to short right field near the foul line, shortstop Joe DeMaestri moved to the normal second base position, Hector Lopez, the third baseman, played in short center field, Johnny Groth, the center fielder, moved to deep left center, Harry Simpson, the right fielder, played in deep right center and left fielder Enos Slaughter played a deep third base. It was bizarre and it created controversy.

Mickey thought the shift was crazy. He wasn't alone. Boudreau was giving Mickey the outfield corners and the left side of the infield. He was daring him to bunt. The shift worked at first. Mickey struck out his first two at bats after failing to lay down a fair bunt each time. When the bases weren't empty, Boudreau didn't put on the shift and Mickey hit a two-run, eighth inning home run. In the three-game Kansas City series, Mickey went hitless in four at-bats against the shift. He had four hits in nine at-bats when there was no shift. When the Yankees visited the A's in Kansas City late in June, Mickey went 4-8 against the shift, but all the hits were singles, including a bunt.

The Sporting News led an outcry. In an editorial, the newspaper expressed concern that the shift would cause Mickey to worry too much, which might cause him to go into a prolonged slump. The solution was to pass a rule outlawing "gimmick" defenses, which was ridiculous. Tigers' manager Bucky Harris said he wouldn't use the shift because he wanted to get Mickey out honestly. Marty Marion of the White Sox, who truly admired Mickey, joked around and said he would put one of his fielders in the stands, while Orioles manager Paul Richards said it was easier to simply walk Mickey.

Despite Mickey's great contributions, the pennant race was close. The Yankees swept the Cleveland Indians and Detroit Tigers in the middle of June on a crucial western swing. While the hometown fans wanted their team to win, they realized they were watching something special when they saw Mickey and the Yankees. At the end of the game in which Mickey hit his 27th and 28th home runs at Briggs Stadium, the sprinkler system had to be turned on after the game to prevent fans from mobbing Mickey as he made his way to the clubhouse. Yankees' road games were usually sold out as fans wanted to see, not only Mickey, but Yogi, Whitey, "Moose" Skowron, Andy Carey, and Gil McDougald.

In 1956, Mickey batted .353 with 52 home runs and 130 RBIs, all tops in the majors. His on base average was a magnificent .464 and he slugged .705. I remember how the Yankees fans recited Mickey's .353, Willie's .296 and Duke's .292. Boy, did we love it.

In previous seasons, fans had anticipated seeing Mickey do something phenomenal every at-bat or on every fielding chance, but often they were disappointed. In his first five seasons as a Yankee, Mickey's top batting average was .311. The most home runs he hit in a season was a modest 37 in 1955. It was not only the first time he led the league in home runs -- it was only the second time he led *his team* in home runs. But 1956 was different.

If the Yankees needed a long ball, he usually provided it. If the Yankees were trailing by two runs with Mickey leading off the inning, he might work out a walk or drag a bunt between the pitcher and first base for a hit to start a rally. He was the RBI man that could also be the table setter. After all, many forget that Yogi, hitting behind Mickey, batted .298, setting an American League record 30 home runs by a catcher. Bill "Moose" Skowron, who usually batted behind Yogi, hit .308 with 23 home runs and 90 RBIs.

With the passage of time, two things have almost been forgotten. First, for much of the 1956 season, Mickey was chasing Babe Ruth's single season home run mark, a record he would again pursue in 1961 with future teammate Roger Maris. As late as the middle of August, Mickey was five games ahead of Ruth's 1927 home run pace, but in back of everyone's mind, including mine, were the 17 home runs Babe hit in September. Ruth had entered the final month of the 1927 season with 43 home runs. Many players who challenged his record had more at that point in the season, but Babe's 17 September home runs beat back every assault. Mickey hit 13 home runs in August and by the first week of September was still two games ahead of Ruth's pace. Then he went into a slump. By September 10, Mickey was four games behind Ruth's 1927 pace, which effectively ended the chase.

Second, Mickey almost didn't win the Triple Crown because he was putting too much pressure on himself. He was too anxious at the plate and wasn't striding into pitches properly. In the first 10 games of September, Mickey hit an anemic .152, with no home runs or RBIs. Mickey told reporters he wasn't concerned with home runs during his slump.

"I wasn't worried about the homers in that spell. All I wanted to do was hit singles, or even a double now and then. I couldn't even bunt … I just wasn't doing anything good."

Casey Stengel and Yankees' coach Bill Dickey worked with Mickey, who finally broke out of the doldrums. On September 18, when Mickey's extra inning home run beat the White Sox to clinch the pennant for the Yankees, Ted Williams was hitting .355 to Mickey's .350. The Yankees went to Boston for a three game series with Mickey going six for nine to regain the batting lead. Then he pulled his groin right after the Boston series and Casey, wanting to be sure Mickey would be available for the World Series, limited him to pinch-hitting duty for five of the last regular season games.

The RBI lead was also in jeopardy. Al Kaline trailed Mickey by only four RBIs with two games remaining. On the last day of the season, Kaline drove in two runs to finish with 128. Mickey pinch hit for Jim Coates in the ninth inning and managed a ground ball that knocked in Jerry Lumpe for his 130th RBI.

Mickey was ecstatic. "That last week or so I was very conscious of it. To tell you the truth, I even dreamed about it at night. The last few days I kept telling myself I had better not get into another fuss like this, because it certainly was nerve-racking."

"Winning the Triple Crown was more important to me than breaking Ruth's record."

"Another reason he wanted to win the batting title was that no switch hitter had ever done it."

It seemed that Mickey did something spectacular every day. His face was on a *Time Magazine* cover and he was the toast of Madison Avenue. He won the first of his three Most Valuable Player awards as he competed with another good-looking kid for the heart, mind, and soul of America … a kid named Elvis Presley.

The Yankees won the 1956 pennant by nine games over the Indians. They faced Brooklyn in the World Series, seeking to make amends for their World Series loss to the Dodgers the previous season. The 1956 Series followed the same strange pattern as the 1955 Series in which the home team won each of the first six games and then lost the seventh.

In 1955, the Series opened in the Bronx where the Yankees won both games. When the fall classic moved to Brooklyn, the Dodgers swept all three games at Ebbets Field. Back at the Stadium, the Yankees won the sixth game, but Sandy Amoros prevented Yogi Berra from being a hero in the deciding seventh game when he made a catch in left field that allowed Johnny Podres to shutout the Yankees. It is rarely mentioned, but Mickey missed most of that Series, batting only 10 times. His substitutes (no one *replaced* Mickey Mantle), Bob Cerv and Irv Noren, managed only 3 hits in 32 at bats.

In 1956, the Series opened in Brooklyn and the Yankees had a fairly healthy Mickey Mantle coming off his Triple Crown season. This time Brooklyn won the first two games, the Yankees swept the next three in the Bronx and the Dodgers won the sixth game at Ebbets Field. The next day, to complete the same pattern as in 1955, the Yankees shutout Brooklyn behind Johnny Kucks.

Yogi hit two home runs off Don Newcombe, Elston Howard hit a solo shot, and Bill Skowron finished it off with a grand slam en route to a 9-0 victory and the Yankees 17th World Championship. Mickey had a decent Series, batting .250, but he hit 3 home runs in the seven games and had a .667 slugging average.

Returning to the video session, the Yankees' locker room, Mickey, and Bob Costas, I was unaware of how quickly the time had passed. It was not surprising, since the atmosphere would have been intoxicating to any baseball fan, making it easy to imagine how I, a Yankees fanatic (me) and a Mickey Mantle nut (Bob Costas), felt. This was fun.

As we wrapped up the video, Greer came over. "Why don't we get together for dinner one night?" She'd spoken to Kathleen on the phone and they had developed a nice rapport.

"Oh, yes," I blurted out. I then thought to myself, "Double date with Mickey Mantle. What a concept!"

CHAPTER 7

DINNER WITH NUMBER 7:
MY FRIEND MICKEY

The limousine carried Kathleen and me over the Triboro Bridge (now the Robert F. Kennedy Bridge) with its lights brightly sparkling for the holidays. We were on our way to the posh Regency Hotel on Park Avenue to meet Greer and Mickey at his apartment. The 45-minute trip seemed to take forever as I reflected on how Mickey Mantle was straight from central casting -- blond hair, blue eyes, and a Herculean body. I thought of having been in Yankee Stadium with Mickey. I had undergone an amazing transition, from sitting in the far reaches of the grandstand as a 12-year-old, to being on the Yankee Stadium field and then from sitting on the bench in the dugout to working in the Yankees' locker room with Mickey Mantle. It was an impossible fantasy that had been transformed into reality.

When we arrived at the Regency the front desk manager directed us to the house phone. We crossed the elegantly furnished lobby; dialed Mickey's number and Greer instructed us to "Come on up." As we got out of the elevator, the door to Mickey's apartment opened. A now-familiar figure stood in the doorway, making it appear narrower that it was. At the age of 59, he was as impressive as ever. It was easy to see that he still retained the enormous power that he had as an active player. Mickey's handshake was that of a man who knew he was in charge, but his face revealed some of the ravages of his post-baseball lifestyle.

Upon entering, Greer told us to make ourselves at home as she directed us to the sofa. We sat down as Mickey opted for the recliner. Mickey and the chair were good friends. Not being completely at ease, I tried to make small talk about "loving Christmas." Immediately I realized it was a mistake.

Into my mind raced a newspaper headline declaring that Billy Martin had been killed in an automobile accident on Christmas day, 1989. I should have thought before I opened my mouth. When a person is confident in someone's company, remaining silent is not a problem; but to me, Mickey Mantle was still not yet just another person. It was too late. Mickey replied that he hated Christmas because as a youngster, he never got any toys at Christmas, and more importantly, Billy Martin had died on Christmas Day.

Greer broke the tension by asking Mickey to make us a drink. What else is new? Kathleen's request of white wine was no problem, but Mickey struggled with my vodka and tonic. He acted like a kid taking a test for which he hadn't studied. "Where's the vodka? Where's the tonic?" It struck me that though Mickey never turned down a drink; he rarely had to mix them. Kathleen noticed the amused look on my face as she gently poked me.

Kathleen and I sat on the couch and provided updates on our kids, Christine, Luke and Laura. Mickey appeared interested but seemed melancholy. I thought that my Christmas mistake triggered Mickey's mood, which was true, but it ran much deeper. Few fans realize the toll being a baseball player takes on family. From the middle of February until the middle of October, Mickey was away from home. He rarely saw his children or Merlyn, and when he did see them, the Yankees' fortunes were always in back of his mind. Mickey didn't leave the game at the ballpark. Although he was often otherwise engaged, he took the game more seriously than most players. Losses grizzled at his psyche and he would sometimes sit silently in front of his locker for long periods of time after a tough defeat. Most of the writers knew enough to leave him alone.

Mickey regretted not being a good dad and not being around often enough. "Sometimes I used to cry when I had to leave for spring training. I would go days during the season without even speaking to the kids. I was almost never there when it counted, and even during the winter, there were banquets and dinners."

There wasn't too much for me to say. Kathleen pointed out that a lot of businessmen spend an inordinate amount of time away from their families. Mickey merely nodded. Nothing could lessen his guilt. I realized that my childhood hero had many of the same problems as I had, but they were more intense. My thoughts were interrupted when Greer asked where we wanted to eat. Mickey slowly snapped out of his funk as we decided to have Chinese food.

Back in the company-provided limousine, we sped past the glorious Rockefeller Center Christmas Tree to Mick's favorite Chinese restaurant, Tse Yang on the East Side. As we approached the restaurant, I fantasized that everyone I had ever known would be seated in the restaurant when I, the kid from Yonkers, walked in with Mickey Mantle. We were escorted to the back of the restaurant behind both a wall and a screen so that Mickey would not be interrupted while eating.

Mickey and Kathleen got along well, in great part because being with a celebrity never fazed Kathleen while Mickey found that not being treated like Mickey Mantle was a pleasant change of pace. Being famous has its rewards, but celebrities often find being treated as an individual can be a novelty. Kathleen vaguely remembered her dad talking about some player named Mickey Mantle during her childhood, but she was never in awe of him.

They started discussing films. Mickey said that *The Last Picture Show* was his favorite all-time movie, which made sense. *The Last Picture Show* told the story of a declining small Texas town during the early 1950s. It was shot in black and white in Archer City to emphasize the bleakness and hopelessness of the town and its people. During almost the entire film, the soundtrack was full of early 1950s country western songs. I still listen to the Hank Williams Jr. rendition of "*Why Don't You Love Me Like You Used to Do.*" Archer City was the hometown of Larry McMurtry, upon whose novel the film was based and with whom I would cross paths when my company, *Cabin Fever Entertainment*, secured the video rights to *Lonesome Dove*, his Pulitzer Prize winning novel.

The Last Picture Show is told from the perspective of an 18-year-old boy whose generation had little to look forward to, based on their parents' and grandparents' past history. The film is a character study that chronicles the mediocre, aimless, shallow lives of the townspeople. It has the simple honesty that Mickey possessed when he came to New York in 1951 as a 19-year-old whose only hope of escaping the Oklahoma zinc mines was to make it as a baseball player. Mickey could have been a character in *The Last Picture Show*. Upon second thought, he *was* a character from the film.

Kathleen asked Mickey what stood out in his mind from his childhood years. Mickey told her that he enjoyed being with his father, although it wasn't all fun and games. He recalled when he was five-years-old, he was forced to bat right-handed against his father, who was a left-hander, and left-handed against his grandfather, who was right-handed, because his father, Mutt, thought that it would give him a big advantage batting. I think Mickey lost Kathleen when he told her that a right-handed pitcher's curve ball breaks away from a right-handed hitter, while a left-handed pitcher's curve breaks away from a left-handed hitter. By switch-hitting, curves to Mickey would always break toward him.

Mickey talked about another film, *What's Eating Gilbert Grape*, which is set in the small town of Endora, Iowa. The protagonist, Gilbert Grape, must choose between duty to his family or escaping from the town. Gilbert Grape had a mentally handicapped younger brother, Arnie, and an obese, 500-pound mother who gave up on life after her husband committed suicide. While Mickey certainly identified with the town of Endora, as I listened, I realized that it was Arnie, not the town that affected him.

Young Mickey had not been torn between remaining with his family in Commerce or becoming a professional baseball player -- his family encouraged him to leave. But Mickey the father identified with Gilbert Grape. He told Kathleen that the extremely vulnerable and challenged Arnie reminded him of his youngest son Billy, who suffered from heart problems and Hodgkin's disease, the latter having killed Mickey's grandfather, father and two of his uncles.

Mickey was a sensitive individual with an intellectual depth that was rarely recognized. The baseball writers accepted his shyness at first, but it was something that Mickey never lost, despite becoming a sophisticated New Yorker. It's a shame that the writers and fans incorrectly interpreted his insecurity and shyness as aloofness. Billed as the next coming of Babe Ruth plus having to take over from Joe DiMaggio in center field only added to the pressures. Until his breakout Triple Crown 1956 season, Mickey was considered a disappointment. Even then, Mickey was booed until Roger Maris joined the team in 1960. Mickey was quoted as saying to Roger, "You've gotten all my fans."

During the meal, we talked a lot about country music, which I loved and knew a lot about. Mickey's life was, in many ways, one of extremes. He became animated when he told the story of the time his good friend, country singer Jim Reeves, a former baseball player, explained how he'd strike him out if he were pitching to him. Mickey said that Reeves told him exactly where he would make each pitch and that when Reeves was finished, "All I could say," Mickey told us, "was that 'Jim, you're right. That sure is my weakness. How did you know? How many of your records am I going to have to buy to keep you from telling anybody else?'"

But then Mickey's mood changed as he recalled that Jim Reeves died at the age of 41 in a plane crash near Nashville. Reeves was piloting a small plane that had left Batesville, Arkansas for Nashville in order to finalize a business deal. A violent thunderstorm developed as the plane approached Nashville, snaring the small aircraft in its crosswinds. Reeves became disoriented, flew the plane upside down, and thinking that he was heading up, flew the plane directly into the ground. All the joy of the first Jim Reeves anecdote was gone. Mickey shifted restlessly as an awkward silence filled our table.

More food arrived and I chirped in with a question about Teresa Brewer, hoping that Mickey would bite. He did. "Man, she was so little and had such a loud voice." I wasn't finished. "Mickey, did you know that she wrote your song?" Mickey looked at me quizzically. "What are you talking about?" I knew I had him. "Mickey, what *is* your song? "I Love Mickey," right? Well guess who wrote it. Right. Teresa Brewer because she really did love you." Mickey just laughed the way he always did. I felt better and continued.

"Mickey, do you have a favorite artist?" Mickey responded that he had a lot of favorites, including Jim Reeves, Teresa Brewer, Roy Clark and Hank Williams. A few years later, when I asked him the same question, he gave a different, surprising answer. "Did you ever hear of Elwood Bunn and the Country Jubilee?" Of course, I hadn't, which seemed to please Mickey the way discovering something great that no one else knows about pleases the discoverer. Mickey could let me in on the secret.

"Elwood is great. He didn't start playin' music until he was about 40 years old. He plays Hank Williams, Eddy Arnold, George Jones, Ray Price, Merle Haggard, Little Jimmy Dickens, Tom T. Hall and Johnny Cash. Whitey took me to see him with Yogi and wouldn't you know it. We met Stan Musial there – in New York. Bluegrass, me, Yogi, Whitey, and Musial, all in New York."

Mickey said that if someone told him way back in 1951 that his favorite country singer would come from New York, he would have told the guy to "stop puttin' me on." While talking, Mickey got a glint in his eye and mentioned the term "peck sack." He wanted to find out just how much we two New Yorkers knew about the "boondocks."

"Tom, what's a peck sack?" He had me. He knew it. Kathleen, who tried to help, was of no help. He couldn't believe that Kathleen and I didn't know what a "peck sack" was. For the uninitiated, or those not from rural Oklahoma, a "peck sack" was used by miners to carry ore from the mines.

As we sat at the table, Mickey wanted to play a numbers game with Kathleen. He said, "I'm thinking three numbers. If you guess them, I'll treat for dinner." Kathleen played along and I prompted her to go with five, three, and six, Mickey's career home run total.

"Wrong! Three, four, five," revealed Mickey. "The retired numbers of Ruth, Gehrig, and DiMaggio." He seemed surprised we didn't guess the correct numbers. At that point, he whipped out one of the postcard drawings of himself and signed, "To Kathy, Thank you Dummy, Mickey Mantle, 3,4,5."

Kathleen and Greer had a lot in common besides their brains and blonde good looks. Both were teachers. Greer had been an elementary school teacher in North Carolina when she met Mickey during one of his promotional appearances. She easily made the transition from managing 25 children to managing Mickey's various business and speaking engagements. Greer gave Mickey a zinger at dinner when she said that "Mick's behavior kept her employed and in contact with childish behavior!"

While Kathleen and Greer discussed teaching, Mickey and I talked about country music some more. He loved Patsy Cline and Roy Clark, and still remembered the melodic sounds of Bob Wills and Ernest Tubbs from his Oklahoma boyhood days. Mickey was friendly with many country stars that he had met at golf tournaments over the years. He told me that Tanya Tucker, whom I had also met, was a regular at his restaurant. He added that she even took a liking to my cowboy boots.

I relayed how my Sicilian grandfather, "Mac", was responsible for my love of country music. Mickey got a kick out of hearing how "Mac" and I would drive around Yonkers, New York in a red pick-up truck, playing and singing along to the country radio station. We would stop at a local pub, "Mac" would get a beer and a shot, and I would get a sarsaparilla. When he took me to the old Madison Square Garden to hear Gene Autry sing "Ghost Riders in the Sky," I was hooked. Because of *Cabin Fever Entertainment's* involvement in several Nashville projects, I was elected to the Board of Directors of the Country Music Association. Greer & Mickey were really pleased when I extended an invitation for them to attend the Association's nationally televised annual awards show.

By now, Mickey was feeling pretty "loose." I never would probe about Mickey and other players, but he sometimes liked to tell me about things he usually didn't talk about. The subject of Yogi managing in 1964 came up. Yogi had replaced Ralph Houk as manager, with Houk moving to the front office as general manager. The Yankees struggled under Yogi most of the 1964 season, with the famous Phil Linz harmonica incident the low light of the year. After losing a four game set in Chicago in late August, the team was on the bus that was taking them to O'Hare airport.

Phil Linz, a utility infielder, sitting in the back of the bus, was bored. He took out a harmonica and started playing "Mary Had a Little Lamb." Yogi, who was sitting in the front and who didn't take kindly to being swept in Chicago, told Linz to knock it off, but Linz wasn't sure of what he heard, so he asked Mickey.

Without having been there, but knowing Mickey, I could see the glint in his eye and the small smile on his face that he tried to hide. Mickey had the chance he wanted. After a pregnant pause, he responded, "He said play it louder."

Mickey broke out in a giggle. Greer rolled her eyes, as Kathleen, who was unfamiliar with the famous incident, became a little puzzled. Mickey stopped chuckling and looked at me, probably wondering why I was quiet. "Tom, I couldn't help myself. It was too good an opportunity to pass up and Yogi was so serious."

"Tom, it was only August 20. We still had almost six weeks left and we were only four and one-half games out. I didn't start in any of the games because I had hurt my knee sliding back into first base a few days before against the Orioles. If I had played, we probably wouldn't have lost all four games. We knew that we were better than the White Sox or Orioles. We knew that we could win. Yogi was so funny. I knew he was serious, which is why it was funny. I couldn't help it. When Phil asked me what he said, I had to do what I did. It loosened everyone up."

The waiter brought us the check. Because we hadn't guessed Mickey's three numbers, I paid, as usual. We returned to the Regency and went to the bar. Greer spotted three or four "eyeballer's" at the far end as we went to our table. "Just a matter of time," she remarked. Sure enough, first the bug-eyed stares, then the toasts. "Mick, you were the best! Mick, you were my idol!" Then the zombie-like walk over to our table for Mickey to sign their napkins.

I resented their intrusion into Mickey's time because it was also an intrusion into my time with him. What a joke that was. I resented something that probably had happened to Mickey several times a day, if not hourly, his entire adult life. He was amazingly cordial.

Jim Bouton, in *Ball Four*, described Mickey as equally capable of ignoring autograph seekers, including children, or going out of his way to mingle with and sign for them. The media emphasized the negative, but most of the time, Mickey was cooperative. People tend to forget that Mickey was a country boy and that country boys are wary of pushy strangers. Greer played the bad cop, "Okay, enough guys."

Bouton's *Ball Four* was a groundbreaking book that revealed the inside baseball culture to the public. People often forget or never even knew that Bouton wrote the book with baseball writer Leonard Schecter or that Bouton revealed that after his first Yankees' win, it was Mickey who laid out a "carpet" of towels leading from the clubhouse entrance to Bouton's locker.

As a kid, I remember reading a column by Schecter after Mickey's 1959 season, which was considered terrible at the time. Mickey hit .285, hit 31 home runs and drove in 75 runs. For the first time in six seasons, didn't walk at least 100 times. Schecter wrote that Mickey, who was a natural right-hander, subconsciously resented having to hit left-handed against his grandfather. For some reason that Schecter couldn't explain, the psychological disturbance manifested itself during the 1959 season. I wonder why it didn't bother him in 1956?

Mickey had a pretty good 1960 season, but he was still criticized for his strikeouts and especially for batting only .275. Overall, he hit .275/.399/.558 with a league leading 40 home runs, but he drove in only 94 runs, struck out 125 times and walked 111 times.

In 2011, MVP candidate Curtis Granderson had an outstanding season. Upon analysis, it was eerily similar to Mantle's 1960 season. Granderson hit .262/.364/.552 with a league leading 119 RBIs. He struck out 169 times while walking 85 times. The Yankees, the fans and Granderson were extremely satisfied with his production. If Granderson had played in 1960, the major criticism would have been that he hit only .262. By the way, Granderson set a new strikeout mark for any Yankees batter with 169 whiffs.

When Roger Maris set the current single season home run record of 61, he was criticized for hitting only .269. Maris struck out only 67 times while walking 94 times. Opposing pitchers couldn't walk Maris with Mantle batting behind him. Maris didn't receive a single intentional walk that year.

In his greatest home run season of 1998, Mark McGwire, who was remorseful about using illegal substances, was walked intentionally 28 times. Barry Bonds, whom some admire for never being remorseful, had 35 intentional passes in his best home run season, 2001.

Mantle hit 40 of the 1960 Yankees' 193 home runs (or 21 percent). Granderson hit 41 of the Yankees' 222 home runs (or 18 percent). Mantle's Yankee Stadium was a more difficult park for home runs than Granderson's home park: the new "Yankee Stadium." In addition, Mantle batted right-handed against lefties, forcing him to contend with Yankee Stadium's "Death Valley" in left-center field. Granderson's 2011 season supports the idea that Mantle's 1960 season didn't deserve the criticism it received.

The changed game as well as modern statistics have revealed that Mantle's sub-par seasons of 1959, 1960 and even 1967 (.245/.391/.434) were better than believed at the time. Mantle was lambasted in the media for striking out 111 times in 1952. The emphasis wasn't on his .311 batting average or on his .394 on base average. In 1952, no one knew that Mantle had led the league with a .924 OPS because the statistic wasn't created until 1984.

Kathleen realized, as we spent more time with Mickey, that I was not unique with my Mickey Mantle memories and home run stories. Intense baseball fans' lives and the game are so intertwined that when someone mentions the 1964 World Series, an image of Mickey hitting a game winning home run off Barney Schultz appears. Fans are immediately transformed back to October 10, 1964. They not only remember the home run -- they remember what they did after the home run and all the other details of their lives linked to the game. Kathleen was so perceptive when she referred to Mickey Mantle fanatics as a cult. It was an entire generation of boys and girls grown to adults whose minds went back in time at the mention of Number 7. It was a common bond that was a hallmark of their childhood.

A few weeks later, I took Mickey to Josephina's restaurant that my cousin Jeffrey had recently opened near Lincoln Center. Mickey was unpretentious and despite having adapted to big city life, he had some problems with the menu. There were many fancy "healthy food" dishes that he couldn't pronounce. I knew how Mickey felt because I prefer steak houses or diners to four-star restaurants that provide small portions for outrageous prices. After that, we skipped the fancy restaurants, making good ol' steak houses our choice.

I'll never forget those dinners with Mickey. He was a humble man with a great sense of humor. As unbelievable as it seemed to me, I often forgot that Kathleen and I were double dating with *Mickey Mantle*. When he was out of the purview of his fans, he was relaxed, funny and great to be around. During those times, Mickey was unassuming, loved to kid with friends and was brutally honest. He was someone Kathleen and I enjoyed being with. The only negative was that he was extremely self-centered in that most of the conversations revolved around Mickey Mantle.

As we all know, Mickey's temper sometimes got in the way. It was worse than even Paul O'Neill's, which has become legendary. O'Neill was roundly criticized for kicking objects, throwing towels out of the dugout, and attempting to destroy his bat when he didn't live up to his own expectations. When I watched O'Neill throw a tantrum, I couldn't help but be reminded of Mickey.

Baseball writers and photographers considered Mantle uncooperative. He occasionally refused to talk to reporters after a poor game, which is unacceptable today. Mickey's teammates were another matter. They regarded him with awe and had genuine affection for him.

Then Mickey's mood changed as we pulled up to the Regency. He told me that something happened when he was a rookie that he would always regret. He related that a Yankee fan named Mrs. Blackburn had a box next to the Yankees dugout. She often gave him gum or some candy as he walked to the on deck circle. She was in a perfect position to hear Mickey's cursing and profanity when he returned to the dugout after striking out.

"After a while Mrs. Blackburn stopped giving me the gum and candy. When she finally couldn't stand the cursing any longer, she started to scream at me. I was really embarrassed." "Stop that talk."

I was extremely angry at the time because I had just struck out again. I yelled back without thinking.

"Shut your goddamn mouth."

I was shocked, but quickly realized that at 19, Mickey had a long way to go controlling his temper.

"It was something I regretted the moment I said it, but it was too late. I thought that she would never speak to me again. Then, a few days later, she added, 'Any more outbursts like that and I'm going to make a personal protest to Mr. Topping.'" Dan Topping and Del Webb were the Yankees owners.

I paid for most of our dinners but Mickey did make amends. He would take all the bills out of my wallet and write X-rated comments. One $20 bill simply says, "To Tom, Tough Shit Asshole, Mickey Mantle." He told me they would increase in value and pay for the dinner. Time proved that he was correct.

Author serving as bodyguard as Mickey signs yet another autograph. He joked that St. Peter would probably ask him to sign a ball at the pearly gates.

Two grown men (Bob Costas & Tom Molito) who idolized #7 as kids, in the sacred Yankee locker room.

Three Icons who hit 1169 Home Runs ... #s 7, 8 and 9 (Mantle, Yogi, Roger Maris)

Mickey about to introduce music icon Charlie Daniels to the Yankee Stadium throng. Two "good ole boys" who hit if off immediately and stayed friends till Mickey's passing.

The great Mickey Charles Mantle. Like Elvis, Marilyn Monroe and JFK
– they only pass our way but one time.

Me and Mickey having lunch in his restaurant on Central Park South in New York City. Photos of 500 Home Run Club members in background.

Two former Italian M.V.P.s. One 1956 Yonkers Little League; the other 3-time American League MVP ... the beloved Yogi Berra.

(Mickey Mantle & Jerry Garcia in one feature)
"I hated the Yankees, but I loved Mickey Mantle!" ~Bob Sullivan, Executive
Publisher at Life Magazine

Me & Roger Maris. Remarkably, Roger still holds the American League Home Run
record (61) 55 years later, no steroid era has toppled it.
He left us way too early…a good man.

CHAPTER 8

SAD NIGHT AT THE WALDORF ASTORIA

After the "500 Home Run Club" video shoot, I returned to my office and the Mickey-less world of budgets, strategic planning and human resources, to discover that there was an interesting request on my desk. Could I arrange for Mickey to appear at the Miami Project to Fight Paralysis? This was an extremely worthwhile event whose goal was to raise awareness and money for spinal cord injuries. Ten superstar athletes were invited and individuals or groups could purchase a table to be seated with the athlete who headed that table.

I called the Regency Hotel and left a message with Greer. At this point, I always dealt with Greer. Although I respected her business role, the truth is that I was afraid I would still come across like a bumbling idiot if Mickey answered. The next day, my secretary, Denise, called into my office. "Mickey Mantle is on line one." What a great adrenaline rush! In the future, when Mickey called my office, Denise would announce the call -- at my urging -- as loud as decorum would permit. The little kid in me wanted every Vice President on the floor to hear her voice because in my mind, their calls from stockbrokers, bankers and lawyers were trivial in comparison. Denise was my right hand "man". She developed strong, personal relationships with the many celebrities I worked with. I could not have functioned without Denise Bucci Iobbi: pretty, smart & tough.

I picked up the telephone and made some small talk with Mickey. I learned over the years that he didn't react to subtleties, irony or quips in conversation. Mickey wanted his conversation black and white, straightforward, and above all, honest. An insincere person would have a difficult time talking to Mickey because any conversation or relationship would end very quickly if it were based on "spin," or if he thought someone were not being up front. He had learned the hard way from his early dealings with unscrupulous individuals who wanted a piece of his fame. This part of his personality contradicted his fondness for constantly putting other people on.

I recall when Mickey was a guest on the Howard Stern Show during the early 1990s. Stern, being Stern, tried to engage Mickey in sexually explicit stories and gossip. Mickey quickly became quite annoyed. He gently, but firmly, told the host that he would rather discuss his new book. Mickey's tone was dead serious and, excuse the pun, stern. Howard, who might have been a little taken aback, focused their conversation on Mickey's book. Verbal jousting was not a good idea when talking with Mickey Mantle.

Mickey agreed to appear at the Miami Project to Fight Paralysis. He expressed empathy for the tragedy of spinal cord injury and the quest for a cure. I was relieved that he'd had such a positive attitude. One of our corporate lawyers had gotten involved in the event and told me Mickey had to come because he was bound by contract to make five appearances at company events, but knowing Mickey, there is no doubt that he would appear because he wanted to help.

When the night of the black tie event arrived, Kathleen and I picked up Mickey and Greer at the Regency. A light dusting of snow covered the pavement as we drove through the brightly lit streets of Manhattan. We arrived at the Waldorf Astoria and amid a buzz of conversations among the guests at the tables we passed, which we could easily tell were about Mickey. Snaking our way through the crowd, we were ushered to our elegant candlelit table. This was Mickey's domain -- 40, 50 and 60-year-old men who grew up at the altar of Yankee Stadium and worshipped "the Mick."

"Hey Mick, how ya feeling?"

"You were the best."

We settled in as I glanced at the two adjacent tables. Directly behind me was Muhammad Ali. To our right were O.J. Simpson and one of the most striking blondes I have ever seen, Nicole Brown Simpson.

The dinner kicked off and the various legends were introduced, despite the fact that none of them needed an introduction. The athletes included

Frank Gifford, Arnold Palmer, Bob Cousy, Bobby Orr, Rafer Johnson, Billy Jean King, Eddie Arcaro, O.J. Simpson, Muhammad Ali and Mickey. Each was asked to stand at his or her respective table. When it was Mickey's turn, he responded with that "aw shucks" country boy grin and a wave, which was vintage Mickey.

Our table consisted of representatives of a Fortune 500 company whose CEO had made a substantial contribution for his group to be seated at Mickey's table. As I sat there and looked at them, I thought about how sports can be the great equalizer among individuals from different economic and social backgrounds. Most of the executives seated at Mickey's table made more money than he did, but baseball gave him attraction and power that none of them could ever know. It was they who contributed to sit with Mickey, not the other way around.

Mickey was quite at ease, probably too much at ease as he simultaneously kidded around with the executives and emptied a bottle of wine. He had learned to enjoy the adulation he received, which could easily be seen. Almost everyone at the table had a question or two to ask Mickey. They were like a group of teenagers getting to talk to Elvis for the first time. Mickey tried to answer them as politely as possible as each one of them showed real pleasure when Mickey asked them a question.

Seated between Mickey and me, Kathleen looked great in her suede suit, but I could sense that she was getting a little perturbed. "He's rubbing my leg!" she whispered to me. Mickey claimed he liked the feel of her suede skirt, but was in fact rubbing her knee. I didn't know what to do or say. I wasn't in the habit of letting other men rub my wife's knee, not even Mickey Mantle. My Sicilian DNA produced extreme jealousy and possessiveness. I tried to rationalize, knowing that it was in vain. "Well, he gave me a lot of thrills," was my reply. Looking back, I think it was just Mickey being Mickey many years before individuals such as Manny were being Manny.

Greer knew Mickey well. She could read faces and responses, which saved me from having to figure out my next step. "Mick, that's Tom's wife!" Mickey's consciousness was never raised when it came to women. Too many women had thrown themselves at him for no other reason than his being Mickey Mantle. He grinned at me after Greer's comment. Looking back, I think it was just Mickey being silly. Or was it?

With his "kidding around" behind him, Mickey began to write down some comments for his turn at the podium. He took the short speech seriously since he was well aware of the devastation crippling injuries could produce, ranging from his high school football days up to his current difficulty with his knees. Unfortunately, he was going through a bottle of Chateau Ste. Michelle wine at a brisk clip. Its effects would soon be felt. As he made notes, one of the executives at the table put several baseballs in front of him and told him to sign them. I immediately knew that we were in trouble.

"Screw You" was Mickey's surly reply.

My worlds collided. I was an officer of a Fortune 500 Company, which was the major backer of this event. I was also developing a relationship with Mickey. If I pressed him to autograph the baseballs it might have made a bad situation worse. As the blood drained from the guy's face, I took the baseballs. "I'm sorry," I said. "I'll try to get them signed later. Don't ask him again."

Mickey was becoming more intoxicated. He had to use the restroom, which meant that he would be taking a short trip that would expose him to more admirers. Not unexpectedly, Greer asked me to accompany him. On the way to the bathroom, Mickey had baseballs pushed at him to sign. He obliged a few, which relieved me. Finally, for what seemed like an eternity, we entered the restroom. Of course, while he was standing at the urinal, somebody shoved a pen and paper at him. I positioned myself between Mickey and the guy and provided interference for the long trek back to our table. I was starting to understand the extent of Greer's job responsibilities and what it was like to be Mickey Mantle.

Now it was Mickey's turn to speak. My stomach formed a knot for good reason. Because of his condition, and with his history, I was filled with trepidation. Alcohol was not kind to Mickey.

It was a disaster. Mickey started by "recognizing" Billy Martin in the back of the room; only the problem was that Billy Martin wasn't there. For the next several minutes Mickey slurred his words and rambled. Initially there were some uneasy chuckles, but everyone quickly recognized Mickey's state. It seemed as if he would never finish. Finally, after a merciful end, he limped to our table to polite applause, and of course, cheers from the Mantle Cult, as Kathleen would refer to them.

My instincts of self-preservation were emerging. I had taken Mickey to the Waldorf Astoria, which meant that my company could have held me responsible for Mickey's disastrous behavior. I began formulating my

response to my boss the next morning. "Hey, I couldn't tell him to stop drinking. You wanted Mickey Mantle and there were risks. I'm sorry but…."
Greer wanted to get Mickey home. We briefly discussed our promotion schedule for the "500 Home Run Club" as Mickey fell into a deep sleep in the back of the limousine. We arrived at the Regency as Greer tried to wake up Mickey. After some gentle prodding, he looked at Kathleen and me as he stumbled out into the street.

Mickey had acted improperly and embarrassed us, but I was beginning to really understand how deeply he believed that his life would follow the pattern of his grandfather, father, and uncle, all of whom had died young from Hodgkins disease. Drinking was an outlet, albeit one that proved to be, in reality, more harmful than his genetics. Mickey's favorite song was "Yesterday When I was Young" sung by Roy Clark. Reflecting on that night, the lyrics provide some insight on Mickey's post-baseball emotions and actions.

Yesterday — when I was young, the taste of life was sweet as rain upon my tongue.

I lived by night and shunned the naked light of day and only now I see how the years ran away.

So many drinking songs were waiting to be sung. So many wayward pleasures lay in store for me, and so much pain my dazzled eyes refuse to see.

I ran so fast that time and youth at last ran out. I never stopped to think what life was all about…

There are so many songs in me that won't be sung. I feel the bitter taste of tears upon my tongue." "The time has come to pay for yesterday, when I was young.

Written by: Charles Aznavour
English translation by: Herbert Kretzmer

CHAPTER 9

MY CIVIL WAR WITH BILLY MARTIN

Back in my office after the Waldorf fiasco, I felt bad for all parties involved despite knowing that Mickey was touched by the event. Kathleen told me he was crying during the video on paralysis effects, but the alcohol had sabotaged his good intentions.

When I was back at work, Greer called with two requests. Billy and Jill Martin had an idea for a video and wanted to meet me. Greer had told them that *Cabin Fever Entertainment* was a class act and that Tom Molito was a straight shooter.

Billy had appeared in an early *Cabin Fever Entertainment* video, *The Baseball Time Capsule*, which had centered on Barry Halper's world-famous baseball memorabilia collection. Barry Halper was a limited partner in the Yankees who had amassed over 80,000 items, including the uniform Lou Gehrig wore at his farewell speech, an original ticket from the first World Series ever played and Ty Cobb's false teeth. At our first meeting, I was taking notes with a fountain pen, which impressed him. He told me later that using an ink-loaded fountain pen was, in his opinion, a sign that the writer took pride in his work. Barry, unfortunately, passed away in 2005, and his collection was sold for a 12-figure sum.

We had shot the *Baseball Time Capsule* at Barry's house in New Jersey, which semed more like a museum than a house. Books have been written about Barry's collection. I asked to see Mickey's uniform. All the uniforms were displayed on a mechanical moving hanger. There were hundreds of them. When I go into a cleaning store to pick up my shirts, I am impressed at the number of items that pass before the clerk gets to my clothing. Imagine that each of those garments were a baseball player's uniform.

"Do you want to see his rookie uniform (number six to follow Ruth's three, Gehrig's four, and DiMaggio's five), a road uniform, or a home uniform?" There were hundreds of autographed balls and bats. The Halper doorbell chimed, "Take Me Out to the Ball Game," and his swimming pool had a huge Yankee logo, which was only fitting since Barry owned a small piece of the Yankees.

In the earlier video we had produced, Billy had served as a guide in "Barryland" and provided great insights into his Yankee teammates, particularly Joe DiMaggio and Mickey. There were some great cameos by Nolan Ryan, Don Mattingly, and Mickey. In 1995, Mickey lent Barry his final piece of Mantle memorabilia, a surgical glove that the doctor had used to probe a particularly sensitive area below Mickey's waist.

Greer's second request was of a more personal nature. She asked me of I could secure a copy of the video of Mickey's Waldorf speech, hoping that showing Mickey his behavior on tape might help him change his lifestyle or at least make him think twice before abusing alcohol.

Several days later she called again, this time to tell me that a lunch with the Martins had been arranged. She revealed that she had showed "Mick," as she always called him, the tape. Mickey Mantle was furious. "Why the hell are you showing me this, to make me feel bad?" Mickey wasn't ready to face his demons.

In David Faulkner's 1995 book, *The Last Hero, the Life of Mickey Mantle*, Greer had elaborated on Mickey's drinking. "I think he felt he was Mr. Personality when he drank, which he wasn't. To be perfectly honest, I'd never been around an alcoholic before. When I met Mick I knew he drank and it seemed like it got progressively worse. At first I didn't realize there was a problem. Finally, I did realize it, so I'd talk to him. I tried to have an intervention with him, and he would balk at that."

I met Billy and Jill at a favorite "watering hole" of Billy's on the East Side. Jill was an extremely attractive woman who was considerably younger than Billy. She had a business sense with a much harder edge than Greer's. Billy was a "Gunslinger." Dressed in western clothes from his western wear shop in New York City, he had a "street persona" about him that made me feel he wasn't somebody to trifle with. Robert De Niro came to mind.

Billy and Mickey were more than best friends. They were brothers in every sense of the word. Billy, the half-Italian, half-Portuguese man-child, grew up on the tough streets of Oakland, California. His 95-pound grandmother, who according to many friends was tougher than he was, raised him. Greer once told me that Billy Martin never asked Mickey to sign a ball, a bat, or a photo in all the years they were friends, which speaks volumes about their relationship. Billy would never exploit Mickey's popularity for his own monetary gain.

Billy was known for winning and fighting. He excelled at both. As a player and manager he consistently drove his teams to victory with an iron hand, the nerves of a riverboat gambler, and knowledge of the game learned from Casey Stengel. Both Martin and Mantle revered the legendary Yankees' manager as a "second father." Billy and Mickey actually reminded me of "Call" and "Gus," the two main characters in the Emmy winning TV miniseries, *Lonesome Dove*, with which *Cabin Fever Entertainment* had been involved. They were very different in temperament, but loyal to their friendship beyond all else.

I had given Mickey a copy of *Lonesome Dove* to watch, primarily because I thought that the relationship between Tommy Lee Jones (Call) and Robert Duvall (Gus) was similar to his and Billy's. Unfortunately, Mickey said the movie depressed him because Gus died. Considering that none of Mickey's male relatives lived past 40, death loomed large on Mickey's mind. It was a driving force in his behavior, such as during the sad night at the Waldorf Astoria. In his 50s and early 60s, he was often quoted as saying, "If I knew I was going to live this long, I would have taken better care of myself."

Billy sat down and ordered a double scotch. He wanted to do a video explaining why his philosophy of managing worked. The idea seemed like a good concept, considering Billy's record. He soon told the waiters, "Bring me another one of these." A second double scotch soon appeared.

Billy learned under Casey Stengel, who had learned under John McGraw, the great manager of the New York Giants during baseball's early days. All that mattered to Billy was winning. While managing the Tigers in 1973, an inmate at Michigan State Prison whom Billy knew, told him that there was a prisoner who could play in the majors. Billy watched Ron LeFlore play in a prison game. After helping him get a one-day parole, Billy brought him to Tiger Stadium for a tryout. LeFlore became an outstanding player.

Recently, there has big fuss made in the media over the fact that Chicago White Sox manager Ozzie Guillen has revealed that "I've hit people before on purpose. Yes I have, because that's my job. Protect my players." In August 1973, the Detroit Tigers' management fired Billy for ordering his pitchers to throw at hitters.

"I don't want to hurt anybody," Billy told me, "but if a hitter leans over the plate too much, he has to know that the pitcher is going to stop it. There is a difference between a headhunter and a pitcher who claims part of the plate. Ask Jackie Robinson how to handle a headhunter."

Billy was referring to Jackie Robinson's way of retaliating against a pitcher he thought was throwing at him. Jackie would push a bunt down the first base line, forcing the pitcher to field it. As the pitcher picked up the ball, Jackie would barrel into him, knocking him flat while trying to jar the ball loose.

The mention of Jackie Robinson's name got Billy started on the 1952 World Series. He started talking to no one in particular, despite the fact that he was sitting next to Jill and me. As soon as he started, I could see by the look on her face that Jill was going to be bored.

"People remember the catch I made against Robinson, but I hit a three run home run in the second game that was just as important. I only got five hits in that Series, but two of them were in that game after we lost the first game. Mickey got three hits, but I got the big hits. People don't remember that. (Johnny) Mize was the Series MVP, but I did okay."

Martin put the Yankees ahead in the fifth inning when he singled home Gil McDougald. Then in the sixth, Mantle led off with a bunt single. Martin finished the scoring with a three run home run. Not only did Mantle lead off an inning with a bunt single but in the Brooklyn third, with the game scoreless, PeeWee Reese singled with one out, bringing up Duke Snider, who was batting third. The left-handed hitting Duke pushed a bunt down the third base line that Gil McDougald had to eat. After Robinson forced Snider at second, with Reese moving to third, Roy Campanella singled in the hole between Phil Rizzuto and Gil McDougald to give Brooklyn the lead.

I enjoyed listening to Billy as I tried to ignore the fact that Jill was not interested. "When I managed the A's, people thought that I used my starters too much, but they were wrong. A pitcher is paid to pitch. Look at Mike Marshall, who knows a little bit about conditioning. But what really pissed me off about 1981 was not the strike but what the idiotic owners did after the strike. Yeah, they told me that what they were going to do meant that we would make the playoffs, but we didn't have to try in the second half. What they did was stupid."

After the 1981 strike ended, the owners decided that the teams that led their division when the strike ended play would make the playoffs. In 1981, there were two divisions in each league. The division winners would play the League Championship Series, with the winners meeting in the World Series. Billy's A's were leading the Western Division when the strike struck. The A's would play the team that had the best record in the Western Division after the strike—but what happens if the A's win the second half? Do they play against themselves?

"I thought it was stupid," Billy said. "If we won the second half we won nothing. In other words I root for Seattle to win -- root for a team we can beat. I suppose it meant every time we played Seattle or Toronto I should have used my second-line pitchers in order to save my starters for teams I had to beat. That's what they told me."

Billy was right. The integrity of the game was being compromised. The Oakland A's, New York Yankees, Philadelphia Phillies and Los Angeles Dodgers had no incentive to win the second half division title because they already were in the playoffs. Those teams had an advantage because they could set up their pitching rotation and rosters well in advance. Of greater significance, as Billy said, they could, at least in theory, help determine the division winner by trying harder against teams they thought would be a greater threat to them in the playoffs.

Billy started to look a little dazed. He stared at the floor, then at me as he started talking about the Civil War. Billy was a student of the terrible conflagration. He owned a large collection of books on the War Between the States, which became part of a lawsuit after his death when his heirs contested who would receive the profits from auctioning off some of his memorabilia.

As Billy gulped his drink, the topic switched from managing baseball games to managing the Union forces at Gettysburg. Billy was quite animated as he brought to my attention the tactical errors on the Confederate side. For Billy, nothing was worse than a victory lost.

He argued that the Confederacy should have isolated and captured Washington D.C., followed by the destruction of the North's industries and railroads. Martin quoted British Colonel G.F.R. Henderson, who made those points in 1898. I always considered myself quite knowledgeable about the Civil War, but I was duly impressed with Martin's expertise. I told Billy that I now understood Billy Martin the manager much better.

Martin's baseball managing took an equally aggressive approach as his managing of the Civil War. When he was skipper of the Detroit Tigers during the 1972 playoffs, Tigers pitcher Lerrin LeGrew hit Oakland A's shortstop Bert Campaneris with an inside pitch. Campaneris threw his bat at the big right-hander, who took umbrage at the act of aggression. Of course, there was a major brawl in which Martin had to be restrained by his team and the umpires from going after Campaneris. Martin believed strongly in never allowing himself to be intimidated. One his strengths was intimidating the opposition. For him, the Confederacy taking over Washington was analogous to beating his opponent in the World Series, using whatever means possible, and did he ever use any means possible.

Martin stole signs, used the squeeze play, embarrassed his players when necessary (see Reggie Jackson) and told his pitchers to throw at opposing hitters, for which the Tigers fired him in August of 1973. His mistake was that he told what he wanted his pitchers to do to the media.

Martin's reputation as a brawler is well documented. His hatred for former Yankees catcher Clint Courtney and the latter's loathing of Martin has become legendary. In 1952, Courtney was with the St. Louis Browns, who were playing the Yankees. The catcher spiked Martin in the second inning of a game at Sportsman's Park. Martin got revenge. In the eighth inning, Courtney was on first with two outs. He attempted to steal second, which was not a wise move. Courtney was out by a mile, but to be certain, Martin tagged him extremely hard right in his face. Courtney followed Martin after the play was over, but Martin turned around and smashed Courtney in the face.

After being fascinated by Martin's Civil War strategies, I told him that I would send a script for Martin's approval. Jill reminded Billy of an afternoon commitment and asked for the check. It had been a strange but illuminating lunch. I saw how drinking made Billy belligerent, which must have led to many of his physical altercations. Different individuals react in different ways to alcohol. Unlike Billy, Mickey would become morose and melancholy when he drank, although on some occasions, he could become nasty.

I told the Martins that I would send them a script for their input. Shockingly, that script became the basis of *Billy Martin: the Man, the Myth, and the Manager,* produced after Billy unexpectedly perished in a terrible truck accident on Christmas Day 1989. Jill Martin called me the day after the accident. My brother-in-law, Tom, answered the phone. He recalls the event:

We were spending the holiday with the Molito family when the horrendous news came over the TV that Billy Martin had died in a car accident as he was returning to his house. His pickup had slid off his long, hilly driveway, and the force of the impact was bad enough to kill him. As this terrible, shocking news broke, Tommy told me that he had a video project with Billy that was in the works.

The dilemma for Tommy that sad day was based on the fact that he would need to call Jill Martin to find out what she wanted to do about the video. Not wanting to intrude, Tommy decided to wait until after the funeral to talk with her about it. About an hour later, I was in Tommy's home alone when the phone rang. I answered and the caller asked for Tommy, so naturally I asked who was calling. Much to my surprise, she told me it was Jill Martin.

When Tommy returned with Kathleen and my wife, I told them that Jill Martin had called. Tommy was surprised and immediately returned the call. Jill was understandably upset, and the video was just another thing for her to deal with. Tommy talked with her in his easy-going way and basically reassured her that the focus of the video would change from Billy the Manager to Billy's life. He went on to tell her that she would have plenty of input into how the story would be told. He also told her that the plan would be to release the video in time for the season opener. Jill was in agreement with Tommy. When it was released that next spring, the video went on to be a success, well received by Jill and the public as well. It was a pretty good seller."

The video was a tribute that contained many poignant moments. Billy's players were extremely loyal to him. Future Hall of Famer Rickey Henderson had a tough time getting through his segment due to the tears streaming down his face. Henderson, the legendary base stealer, claimed, "I didn't know you were allowed to steal home until I met Billy." Mickey made an emotional appearance on the video, detailing the brotherhood that existed between them as well as how Billy was his best friend in life.

After the video had been produced, we held a press conference for its release at Mickey's restaurant. I introduced Jill, who gave a heartfelt history of the project and answered questions from the press. We had invited Mickey to attend, but Billy's death was still an open wound.

We were promoting other *Cabin Fever Entertainment* videos besides Billy's. After I had conducted some interviews for those in attendance, something really funny happened that was quite silly.

I began to get annoyed at some people asking me if I "wanted any meatloaf." I was taken aback. Why would I want meatloaf? I later discovered that my high frequency hearing loss had prevented me from hearing what they were really saying.

"Do you want to *meet* Meat Loaf?"

Meat Loaf was the rock star whose record, "Paradise by the Dashboard Light" is one of the greatest songs about teenagers coming of age sexually. It uses baseball metaphors to describe steps of progress, with the bases and home plate representing progressively increasing steps of intimacy. Former Yankees' announcer and Hall of Famer Phil Rizzuto announced a portion of a baseball game in the song. I regret not meeting Meat Loaf because, after all, he was the only other slightly overweight person at the press conference, but I did meet a 6'5´ black leather attired shock jock named Howard Stern. To this day, I laugh with Howard Stern every day on his Satellite Radio show.

After the press conference, as I walked to my car, I began to look forward to traveling with Mickey and Greer to promote the *500 Home Run Club*. We had sent an advance copy of the video to the industry trade association and had been awarded "Sports Video of the Year". My life was going well.

A few weeks later, I had some time between meetings and was hungry, which for me, was not unusual. Like most busy individuals, I often am not aware of my location, having to pause a second to regain my bearings. As I looked around, I realized that I was near 59th St. and Central Park South, which meant that I knew where I was going to get some food.

As I entered Mickey's restaurant, I peered around to see if he were there when I felt a hand on my shoulder.

"Tom, how are ya?"

The voice belonged to Mickey. I turned around and we shook hands. He led me toward the back were it was less crowded, as many of the diners followed Mickey with their eyes but did not ask him to sign anything. We sat down as a waitress came over to take our order.

"How is everything?" I asked.

Mickey told me that the restaurant was doing better because he was finally able to talk about Billy's untimely death. I kept quiet as he told me that of all the things that bothered him, he still felt guilty about Billy being traded by George Weiss in 1957. It's funny but maybe it's human nature to pick out one event from a person's life and exaggerate its overall significance. Billy always said that he never got over leaving the Yankees. Mickey became silent. I reacted.

"Sure it made a tremendous difference, but you had nothing to do with it and anyway, George (Steinbrenner) brought Billy back to manage the Yankees and they won the World Series"

"Yeah, but Billy didn't play a long time after (the trade). It never should have happened. He would have played longer if the trade never happened."

I never realized that Martin's playing career ended with the Cincinnati Reds after the 1961 season when he was only 33-years-old. After the trade, in which the Yankees sent Billy, Ralph Terry, Woodie Held and Bob Martyn to the Kansas City A's for Harry Simpson and Ryne Duren, Casey Stengel said that the A's got the better of the deal. Billy cried when he was told he was no longer with the Yankees. He said that he would do anything he could to beat them out of the pennant. Mickey continued.

"Maybe I could have stopped Hank from arguing with that guy. I don't know. We didn't start it but Weiss fined us (Mantle, Berra, Bauer, and Martin were fined $1,000 each, while Johnny Kucks was fined $500) and made it look as if it was our fault. Weiss was looking for an excuse to get rid of Billy. I should have talked to Casey more or done something."

Mickey was trying to blame himself for something over which he had no control. It was Billy Martin's 29th birthday and an unfortunate incident had occurred. I then made a point that I think helped Mickey.

You just said that Weiss was looking for any excuse to trade Billy. Don't you think that if it weren't the fight at the Copa, Weiss would have used something else as an excuse so Casey couldn't object? We both know Billy was always getting in trouble, so he was just setting himself up."

I could see that some of the tension left Mickey's face. I struck a nerve, which made me feel good. The waitress brought our food as Mickey remembered the first game Billy played against the Yankees.

"Billy got two hits in the first game he played against us. I think we won, but he really played like a mad man that day. What was weird was that we were in Kansas City and he just switched locker rooms. I'll never forget the look on his face his first time up. He didn't get a hit, but he singled next time up. Billy would have been traded no matter what." Mickey chuckled, got a glint in his eye, and said, "Ask Reggie."

"Reggie" was Reggie Jackson and Mickey could have been referring to any number of confrontations between Billy and Reggie. I often wondered about that first game that Billy played for the Kansas City A's so I looked up the box score. What I realized when I looked at the Kansas City batting order was unbelievable. Every player in the A's order that day either played for or would play for the Yankees.

Kansas City Athletics Batting Order
1. Vic Power 1B Traded to A's in 1953.
2. Billy Martin 2B Traded to A's in 1957.
3. Irv Noren RF Traded to A's in 1957.
4. Bob Cerv CF Sold to A's in 1956.
5. Lou Skizas LF Traded to A's in 1956.
6. Hal Smith C Traded to Orioles in 1954. Traded him to A's in 1956.
7. Hector Lopez 3B Traded to Yankees in 1959.
8. Joe DeMaestri SS Traded to Yankees in 1959
9. Tom Morgan P Traded to A's in 1957.

Kansas City Athletics' owner Arnold Johnson had purchased Yankee Stadium and Blues Stadium, the home of the Yankees' top minor league farm team, in 1953, prior to becoming the A's owner. To avoid any appearances of impropriety, Johnson sold Yankee Stadium back to the Yankees when he became a baseball team owner. Johnson had many business relationships with the Yankees which prompted many accusations that the A's were a "Yankees' farm team." As a Yankees' fan, I always defended the trades made between the Yankees and Kansas City, but as I look at the June 16, 1957 Kansas City lineup, I have to re-think my position.

It was getting late and I still had a meeting to attend. I told Mickey that we would be in touch as I got up to leave. We shook hands. As he sat down again, he thanked me and then, always being Mickey Mantle, told me that I would be getting the check for the meal in the mail. By this time, I was comfortable enough with Mickey to tell him that "Dr." Molito's bill would also be in the mail.

CHAPTER 10

ATLANTIC CITY TO VEGAS

The 500 Home Run Club was off to a great start, winning "Video of the Year." There was a big baseball memorabilia event in Atlantic City, and as luck would have it, many of the 500 Club members would be present. Additionally, the video industry VSDA (Video Software Dealers Association) was due to meet both in New York City and Las Vegas to introduce all the new movies coming out on video in 1989. These three events would launch our product.

Mickey agreed to make appearances at each event, and we made plans to start off at the Jacob Javits Convention Center in New York City. Mickey's appearance went extremely well. Greer later told me, "Mick felt bad" about the Waldorf as well as about any grief he may have caused me. He sincerely wanted to help promote the videos beyond any contractual obligations.

The day started off beautifully as we pulled up to the Javits Center. My brother Ed, who worked in field operations for *Cabin Fever Entertainment*, was there to greet us and show us our booth. Ed was adorned in his best country western clothes, (hat, boots, buckle etc.). He and Mickey had an immediate affinity. "You like country music?" asked Mickey. "Oh yeah," said Ed, as they discussed bass fishing, deer hunting and Willie Nelson.

Comically, another *Cabin Fever Entertainment* employee, Patricia, all five-feet and one-hundred and two pounds of her, decided that she'd be Mickey's bodyguard. As we walked through the giant exhibition area, Patricia "blocked" anyone who came within five feet of Mickey, proclaiming, "Not now. Come to booth 451." Mickey laughed at her aggressiveness as he told Greer, "Learn how to block like that little Patty."

Ed would meet Mickey again years later on a flight. The way he tells it is that he spotted Greer and Mickey in first class. Like me, when I was in the Army, he too was hesitant to approach Mickey. Another co-worker urged Ed on. "He knows you!" Well, Ed raised the nerve to approach first class and as he did, Greer immediately recognized him and waved him up to their seats. "Mick, its Tom's brother." Mickey just stared at Ed. "Mick! Tom's brother," Greer repeated. Mickey kept staring as Ed sheepishly walked away. As Ed left the first class area, Mickey called out, "Where's your cowboy hat?" Mickey the jokester was having fun.

Mickey stayed at the booth well beyond his committed two hours. He signed every autograph requested of him and posed for hundreds of pictures. Mickey concentrated on pleasing the assemblage of media that covered the event. For all his fans, he was exactly the hero they imagined. *The 500 Home Run Club* and *Cabin Fever Entertainment* received great publicity in the newspapers the next day thanks to Mickey's appearance.

There was one poignant moment. A young man placed a photograph of Mickey on the desk for him to autograph. As he carefully signed, Mickey asked the young man his name.

"Bob Furillo," was the response.

Mickey then asked "You're not related to Carl Furillo, are you?"

"Yes, he was my dad" was the response.

Carl Furillo had been an outfielder for the legendary Brooklyn Dodgers teams that often challenged the Yankees in the World Series. He was a fine hitter, a National League batting champion, and an excellent right fielder with a terrific arm that sometimes proved an embarrassment for batters who couldn't or didn't run fast to first base.

Right field in Ebbets Field was not deep. The distance to right center was only 352 feet while the foul line was a hitter-friendly 297 feet from home plate. Many a pitcher hit a hard line drive single to right field, only to have Furillo, who played shallow, race to the ball, pick it up and fire to first base to turn what looked like a single into an out. He didn't do it only to pitchers.

The Ebbets Field right field scoreboard was 40 feet high. Furillo was expert at playing balls hit off the scoreboard, which reminds me about a funny Mickey story when he was a rookie. Mickey asked Casey how to play the right field wall at Ebbets Field. The Yankees' manager told reporters,

"It was the first time the kid ever saw concrete. I explained how the ball hits the wall like this and bounces like this and how you take it as it comes off the wall. I told him 'I played that wall for six years, you know.' He said, 'The hell you did.' He probably thinks that I was born at the age of 60 and started managing right away."

Carl Furillo won the 1953 National League batting title with a .344 average. His lifetime .299 batting average is a point higher than Mickey's. Furillo played 13 seasons then hung on for two more in which he saw limited duty. The "Reading Rifle" was a clutch player who made some great World Series plays and got some key World Series hits.

I was only eight-years-old, but I remember Carl Furillo playing right field in Yankee Stadium in the fifth game of the 1952 World Series. With Brooklyn leading by a run in the bottom of the 11th inning and the Series tied at two games each, Johnny Mize hit a deep drive to right field, where the four-foot-high wall was 344 feet from home plate.

Furillo went back as far as he could on the towering drive with every eye in the ballpark glued on the ball. At the last possible instant, at the only instant in which success could be achieved, Furillo leaped as high as he could, his left hand stretched to its absolute limit. He caught the ball to preserve the Brooklyn win. Boy, was I upset, but it all turned out fine when the Yankees won the Series in seven games.

Furillo had a rough time after baseball, working as a laborer on construction jobs, including one on the World Trade Center. He died young. Mickey stood up to embrace Carl Furillo's son, who was still a young man.

"Your father was a great player and it was an honor to play against him. He was a good man."

I was deeply impressed. Mickey was very gracious to young Mr. Furillo. He exhibited real human warmth. It graphically illustrated how Mickey, like all great competitors, would almost literally want to completely destroy his opponents during the heat of competition, but once the game was over, the intensity was gone until next time. They were opponents but they were friends. In today's game, intensity still exists, but it was not usual to see Derek Jeter pat an opposing player on the back after the opposing player just hit a double. No one wants to win more than Derek Jeter, but today, literally, the players all belong to the same union.

Speaking of shortstops, Mickey was Tony Kubek's all-time favorite ball player. Kubek is one of the most underrated of all New York Yankees shortstops. He played for the Yankees for nine seasons and was a member of three World Championship teams (1958, 1961-62). Kubek found Mantle to be a caring, thoughtful individual to himself personally as well as to youngsters. When Kubek joined the Yankees in 1957, Mantle was coming off his Triple Crown season. Kubek will never forget how he was treated by the best player in baseball.

In 1957, rookies were regarded quite differently from today. In an interview with a Canadian reporter, Kubek, who was the Toronto Blue Jays announcer, revealed how Mantle was instrumental in getting Kubek uniform number 10, which had been Phil Rizzuto's number.

"Back then, rookies could be seen but not heard. There was definite class distinction. When you came to camp as a rookie you got a high number so that there'd be no mistaking you. I got 34. One day after a couple of dozen games, Mantle sat down beside me and called to the trainer: 'Give this kid a low number. He's gonna be around awhile.' They gave me 10 and I wore it for my nine years up there."

Kubek played 882 games at shortstop, but he also played the outfield, third base and second base. He often would play center field when Mantle was injured.

"Sometimes he was in pain. I used to say to him 'For God's sake, don't play. Let that thing heal.' "But he'd say - and, look, there'd be nobody around, he wasn't making a grand gesture - he'd say: 'Tony, maybe there's a guy out there with his kid, and it might be the only ticket he can afford all season, and he brought his kid to see me. So I better be out there.'"

Mantle and DiMaggio had agreed that while they would never be friends, they would always be friendly. At the first Old Timer's Day that the retired Mickey Mantle attended, the public address announcer made a mistake. Instead of DiMaggio being introduced last, the recently retired Mantle was introduced last. Mickey received a bigger ovation than DiMaggio, who was extremely pissed, but Mickey took action. Kubek explained what happened.

"Mantle saw that Joe, a remote guy, a loner, was really offended. Joe told Bob Fishel, the PR guy, that he wouldn't be back. Fishel, at Mickey's prompting, introduced Joe last at all future Old Timer's Days."

Kubek saw many of Mantle's home run. He recalled two that Mantle hit in Washington's Griffith Stadium. No, not the one that allegedly traveled 565 feet off a Chuck Stobbs delivery.

"We were in Washington's Griffith Stadium, a huge park where center field was 420 feet away with a high green wall and, beyond that, a grand oak tree. Camillo Pascual, a right-handed curve baller, was pitching for the Senators when Mantle, batting left, hit a ball into the oak tree. The old catcher, Bill Dickey, who was our first base coach, said he'd seen the Babe put one in that tree too. Three innings later, Mantle came up again, and Chuck Stobbs, a left- hander, was now pitching. Hitting right, Mickey hit the ball over the tree. We all watched Dickey in the coach's box at first base. He stared towards center and then he turned to the bench and put his head down and covered his eyes. He couldn't believe it."

The next promotion for our video was the Atlantic City Convention, which also went well. I got to meet some of the great sluggers of baseball history, including Hank Aaron, Willie Mays, Harmon Killebrew and Eddie Mathews. Observing Mickey and Willie Mays together was interesting. Mickey seemed in his element and relaxed. Mays acted like he couldn't wait to leave Atlantic City. Both Mickey and Willie had experienced major issues caused by the nature of Atlantic City's primary type of business.

Baseball Commissioner Bowie Kuhn told Willie Mays on Oct. 26, 1979 that if he accepted a public relations position with the Bally Manufacturing Corporation, which owned several gambling casinos in Atlantic City, he would be banished from baseball. At the time, Willie worked for the New York Mets as a part-time coach and good will ambassador, positions he would no longer be able to hold if he accepted Bally's offer. Three days later, Willie signed a 10-year contract worth more than $1 million with Bally's to make public appearances (read that as playing golf with the patrons) on behalf of the corporation's new Atlantic City casino.

Kuhn had sent a letter to Bally's outlining his position a full month before Willie was told he would be banished. Neither Willie nor his lawyer knew Kuhn had sent the letter because they never saw it. Willie found out about the possible ban only when Kuhn gave him a week to make up his mind. He was shocked by the ultimatum since he had been working for a corporation that had been in charge of racetracks for the previous five years. Many leading baseball figures, including former Pittsburgh Pirates' owner John W. Galbreath, who named one of his horses after Roberto Clemente, as well as New York Yankees' owner George Steinbrenner, have been intimately involved with the Sport of Kings. Willie was banished from baseball for life.

On February 8, 1983, the Claridge Hotel and Casino announced that Mickey had signed a $100,000 a year contract to become their Director of Sports Promotions. Titles and responsibilities often are different. Like Willie, all Mickey had to do was greet clients and play golf with them. At a press conference, Mickey said, "It's nothing I'm ashamed of. It's not like I'm standing outside the hotel and trying to get people to come in and lose their money. It's primarily the same job I've had since I got out of baseball."

Mickey worked for the Yankees during spring training and reportedly received $20,000. He put on a good front when he spoke to reporters when he announced he had accepted the Claridge job. Mickey later revealed that he had been banished from baseball the previous day. Of course, Commissioner Kuhn, in his statement, reiterated the fact that both Mickey and Willie, while unable to be employed by baseball, "… or continue to be welcome at all baseball functions." Bowie Kuhn was willing to re-interpret his standards if it were to his advantage. Peter Ueberroth became commissioner on March 18. 1985. One of his first acts was to immediately reinstated Mickey and Willie.

After promoting the video, Mickey, Greer, Kathleen, my boss, Tom O'Grady and I met for dinner. Tom was an elderly gentleman with more brains and common sense than any one person should be allowed to have. He was Vice Chairman of the holding company that owned *Cabin Fever Entertainment*, and was equally at home in a corporate boardroom or backstage at a Lynyrd Skynyrd gig.

After dinner, Kathleen and Greer said goodnight, leaving the two Tom's and Mickey to talk very late into the night. Tom O'Grady's Midwest background and Mark Twain type insights appealed to Mickey. I think they reminded him of his roots and particularly of his father, Mutt Mantle. I often wonder what thoughts must have raced through Mutt's mind as he observed Mickey's power and speed as a young teenager.

I saw a side of Mickey that night that talked of farming, zinc mining and the hardships of digging a living out of the harsh Oklahoma land. He discussed his father's family values and work ethic, telling Tom and me that his father was a good man who expressed himself through his actions, not by his words.

"My father was almost always quiet, but he could freeze you with a look. He smoked too much, but he figured that working in the mines all day was more harmful than smoking cigarettes. I sure didn't inherit my drinking from him. All he ever did was bring home a half-pint on Saturday and nurse it along the rest of the week. He would have whipped me if he ever caught me drinking. That's kind of funny, isn't it?" Tom and I just smiled in an embarrassed way, but I can't help but think how scientists have shown that alcoholism is sometimes inherited. That was not true in Mickey's case and the general issue is not yet resolved. Yes, alcoholism often is a family affair, but do youngsters emulate their parents or is alcoholism a parental trait that can be inherited? Regardless, I felt trusted to hear Mickey's revelations. Mutt sounded like a Steinbeck character out of *The Grapes of Wrath*. His death at 39 was still an open wound for Mickey.

Mickey was next scheduled to make the Las Vegas appearance, but he was forced to cancel the trip due to a conflict with a pharmaceutical corporation that was using him to publicize a new arthritis drug. Actually, the company wasn't using Mickey. It was using his injured knees, which were the perfect spokesmen. Since he couldn't go, Greer made the trip to help Mickey out and to have some fun. She had a great laugh, tinged with a little naughtiness which, when coupled with Mickey's X-rated humor, created quite a team, which reminds me of another, quite different team that was managed by an individual with whom Greer related quite well.

Seventy-year old Jay Gigandet managed the great comedy team of Abbott and Costello. He had produced a dog training tape for *Cabin Fever Entertainment* that was hosted by Broadway singing star Howard Keel, which is how we met. Jay Gigandet was old-time Hollywood. He wore white leisure suits and the type of cap worn by guys on motorcycles with sidecars, cursed like a sailor and constantly berated "A Holes" for "Speaking with my damn mouth!" Greer and Jay got along famously.

While we were in Las Vegas, we had had a good Forum to promote the video. I was listening to a national radio broadcast featuring Mickey promoting the *500 Home Run Club*. During the interview, much to my astonishment, Mickey mentioned my name! You can't make this stuff up. I'm sitting in a suite in Las Vegas with Mickey Mantle's girlfriend and Abbott and Costello's manager, listening to Mickey Mantle mention my name on national radio. It had been some trip from the upper deck in Yankee Stadium watching Mickey play as a twelve-year-old to this point in my life.

I returned to my room and the message light was flashing: it was Mickey. "How did you know I can't catch fish?" was the short simple message. I had sent our latest videotape to the Regency the prior week: *How, Where, and When to Catch Bass*.

CHAPTER 11

MICKEY, WILLIE, AND SOME DUKE

Willie Howard Mays Jr., Number 24, roamed the spacious Polo Grounds' center field for much of the 1950s. Every hero must have a villain and my villain, one whom I admired, detested and feared, was the exuberant, stickball-playing outfielder of the New York Giants.

Mickey and Willie were linked from the beginning. Both started their major league careers in 1951 as "can't miss 19-year-old phenoms" after much ballyhoo. Mickey made the Yankees roster after his great spring training, while Willie started the season in the minors, where he excelled. He was called up by the Giants in late May after batting .477 for the Triple-A Minneapolis Millers. Both struggled mightily at first, finding major league pitching a great challenge. Mickey and Willie each had great talent that triumphed over inexperience.

I think that my animosity toward Willie Mays started when he hit a lazy fly ball in the second game of the 1951 World Series between the Yankees and Giants. Playing right field, Mickey caught his spikes in a drainage cover as he and Joe DiMaggio raced for Willie's fly ball. DiMaggio made the catch as Mickey went down like a wounded deer. I know that Willie had nothing directly to do with Mickey's injury, but emotions are funny things. Logically, anyone on the Giants could have hit the fly ball, Willie didn't do anything deliberately to try to hurt Mickey and if the drain hadn't been there, nothing would have happened. But I always associate Mickey's injury with Willie Mays' fly ball.

After an inconsistent rookie year in which he hit .267 with 13 home runs, Mickey had a fine sophomore season, hitting .311 with 23 home runs. Willie, who settled down after a slow start and was the National League

Rookie of the Year in 1951, played in only 34 games in 1952, hitting .236 with 4 home runs until he had to report to the U.S. Army.

I still remember how the baseball magazines and newspapers harped on Mickey's 111 strikeouts, instead of writing about his excellent second season. Willie missed all of 1953 as Mickey was having another good year, but not as good as everyone thought it should have been. It was during the 1953 season that Mickey was often compared to another great New York City center fielder, one who played in Brooklyn.

Edwin Donald "Duke" Snider joined Brooklyn in 1947. He became the Brooklyn Dodgers' regular center fielder two years later. The "Duke of Flatbush" reached his peak in 1953. Duke had a much better year than Mickey, out hitting him, .336 to .295, with twice as many home runs, 42 to 21. In 1953, Duke Snider was ranked as New York's, and probably baseball's, top center fielder.

When Willie returned to the major league scene in 1954, he was greeted like a young paladin who had yet to conquer the baseball world but who soon would do just that. Mickey's .300 average and 27 home runs paled in comparison to Willie's league leading .345 batting average with 41 home runs. To make matters worse, Duke barely lost the batting to Willie, hitting .341 with 40 home runs, which clearly put Mickey third.

The Yankees streak of five consecutive pennants and World Championships ended that year when the Cleveland Indians won an American League record 111 games. In the Senior Circuit, Willie, Don Mueller, Alvin "Blackie" Dark, lefty starter John Antonelli, along with bullpen specialists Hoyt Wilhelm and Marv Grissom led the underdog Giants to the pennant. They swept the record-setting Tribe to win their first World Championship in 21 years.

In 1955, Mickey led the American League in home runs with 37, Duke hit 42, while Willie hit a major league leading 51. Instead of the press lauding Mickey's first home run title, he was criticized for striking out 97 times. Today's player routinely strikes out over 125 times. Who thinks that the game has changed? The fact that Mantle drew 113 walks and had a .431 on base average was virtually ignored. I felt that Mickey was better than Willie or the Duke, but the numbers said otherwise and Mickey had not yet had a breakout season.

Most considered Mays a superior player to Mickey at that time. Brooklyn fans were certain that their Duke was better than either of the two others.

The worst were my neighborhood "friends" and schoolmates who rooted for the New York Giants and Willie Mays. I hated arguing with them, even when I was with my friends who felt as I did about Mickey to back me up. I guess it was because of my neighborhood New York Giants "friends" that I didn't pay that much attention to Snider, who actually had more total home runs and RBIs from 1954-1957 than either Mickey or Willie. The Polo Grounds was much closer to Yankee Stadium than Ebbets Field. I was concerned with Willie Mays.

Then it was 1956. Willie hit .296. Mickey hit .353. Willie hit 36 home runs. Mickey hit 52. Willie knocked in 84 runs. Mickey knocked in 130. Mickey Mantle won baseball's Triple Crown. Mickey was the Major League Player of the Year. Mickey was the American League's Most Valuable Player. Mickey Mantle won the prestigious Hickok Award as the nation's greatest professional athlete of 1956. It was nirvana for me and for all Mickey Mantle fans. Still, the arguments continued, even when Willie moved 3,000 miles away.

The Mantle-Mays-Snider debate in the tri-state region was far more heated and longer lasting than even the debates comparing Babe Ruth to Ty Cobb. Since Duke was older and his skills declined precipitously once the Dodgers were taken from Brooklyn, the argument became Mickey versus the flashy Willie.

I considered it a negative that Willie was a little bit of a showboat in the days when showboating was frowned upon by all but those who pulled for the showboat's team. The newspapers and baseball periodicals explained that was how Willie demonstrated his joy of the game. I always became annoyed when Willie's hat would go flying or by the way he grabbed on to a base that he had stolen. Some fans used to say that Willie deliberately wore a hat that was too large for his head so it would fall off more easily.

Willie was flash while Mickey was modesty. Mickey never played the crowd for reaction. With his head lowered, no smile and sheer intensity on his face, he was the epitome of the competitive ballplayer who took the game seriously. When Mickey did become emotional, it was because he was mad at himself for failing, as many a dented water cooler can verify.

The older, mature Mickey I double dated with was not the Mickey who played for the Yankees. When he was a player, Mickey was often irascible. It has been written that "Mantle must have insulted, offended, or at least irritated every civilized person who met him before he reached the age of 30."

The Mickey I met years later was the opposite. He was humble, vulnerable and was both pleased and a little surprised that people still wanted to meet him. If I didn't know he was Mickey Mantle, I would have never guessed it, but Willie was different.

Well-respected baseball writer Tom Boswell, in *Diamond Dreams*, provides some insights into the differences between Mickey and Willie when their careers were over. Boswell writes that Willie dislikes and resents the intrusive, demanding idol worship from the public that Mickey humbly accepted. Willie acts as if people are trying to steal something from him – his privacy – while Mickey was flattered and even a little embarrassed to take money for signing his name. Willie is often morose and the only times he is the animated kid who played stickball on the streets of Harlem after a Giants' game are the times he is with athletes in a locker room. Boswell writes that Willie is "… funny, sarcastic, profane, giggling uncontrollably, agitating everybody, and is a god among mortals."

As I got older, I realized that Mays' career was at least equal to, if not better than Mickey's, based on Willie's health, longevity and statistics, but I might have been wrong because Mickey's best seasons were superior to Willie's best seasons. I admit that I am biased in favor of Mickey. Isn't that obvious? Many "experts" believe that neither Mickey nor Willie was the equal of another great New York center fielder, Joseph Paul DiMaggio, who in recent years has been the subject of some dubious criticism and analyses which have pushed him behind Mickey in the estimation of many.

According to Boswell, DiMaggio was an approachable, quiet, handsome, gentlemanly Italian man who was naturally reserved and somewhat reticent. The latter two characteristics are not viewed favorably by those in the media. DiMaggio always said that he would rather listen than speak. He respected tradition, enjoyed old friends, family and familiar routines. Fiercely proud of his career, DiMaggio had the natural dignity to know that the great fuss made over him was unseemly. Like Mickey, DiMaggio seemed relieved when people treated him without awe.

Roger Angell, the incomparable baseball writer for *The New Yorker*, wrote that, "You watched Willie play, and you laughed all the time because he made it look fun. With Mantle, you didn't laugh. You gasped."

Allen Barra, a highly respected baseball writer, book reviewer, and social critic for the *Village Voice*, reached the conclusion that Mantle's best years were far superior to Willie's. The *Wall Street Journal* ran an article on June 28,

2002 written by Mr. Barra:

Because both were about the same age, the same size, played the same position in the same city and had virtually the same talent, this is likely the most argued-about duo in baseball history. Over the long haul, the almost never injured Mays was the more valuable of the two. But that isn't the definite answer. Looking at a dozen of each player's peak seasons, I found to my surprise that Mr. Mantle was the superior ballplayer. How did I arrive at this?

Fielding. "Mr. Mays was the far superior outfielder, but not by that wide margin. In center field, he averaged 2.56 fly balls per game, compared with Mr. Mantle's 2.26. But break that down further: every few games, Mr. Mays got a fly ball that Mr. Mantle couldn't or perhaps, never had a chance to get to because Yankee pitchers struck out so many more batters than the Giants."

Base Running. Though Mr. Mays was thought to be better on the base paths, Mr. Mantle may have better used his speed. Mr. Mays led the National League in steals from 1956 through 1959, with 338 out of 441 (for a 76% success rate). The Mick, who was seldom called on to steal, was even more difficult to throw out. He stole 153 bases in 191 attempts, for an impressing 80.1% average.

Batting. The edge is in the batting eye. While Mr. Mays played 591 more games, Mr. Mantle walked 269 more times. His career on-base average of .421 (37 points higher than Mr. Mays) is higher than any modern slugger's including Barry Bonds .419 career average (through June 2002). In their 12 best seasons, Willie Mays played in 128 more games than Mickey Mantle. But the difference is actually greater since Mr. Mays almost always played complete games, whereas Mr. Mantle often appeared as just a pinch hitter when injured. Mantle during those years led in walks (1308 vs. 876), runs (1,421 vs. 1,372), runs batted in (1,311 vs.1198), home runs (481 vs. 426).

In a very special private moment, late at night in his restaurant, Mickey once told me, "When I was not injured, I was better than them all!" I was staggered by this statement from a very humble man as I nodded my head in affirmation. I felt great because in confirmed what I had always believed.

Bill James, the noted baseball statistical pioneer, builds a case that Mantle at his best was a far superior player to Mays at his best. James' conclusion was based on Mickey's ability to get on base and score runs (more on this later).

Mickey led the league in runs six times, second only to Babe Ruth. If you couple his hits with his impressive walk totals, his on base percentage of .421 (lifetime) is mind-boggling.

Willie Mays was the most exciting player of his time, but the most exciting is not always the best. James Bond films are exciting, especially the more recent, but they were not the best films of their era. Driving a Corvette is exciting, but the Corvette was not the best car of its era. And Willie Mays was exciting, but Willie Mays was not the best player of his era. Willie Mays was not Mickey Mantle in my opinion.

With the exception of Babe Ruth, Mickey Mantle had more pure talent than anyone who ever played the game. Mantle hit the ball farther, ran faster and stole bases more successfully than anyone else. His natural talent was so amazing that experienced baseball people who thought they had seen it all were taken aback when they saw Mickey Mantle play.

Hall of Fame shortstop Phil Rizzuto: "I never saw anybody hit the ball so hard. When he swings the bat, you just have to stop and watch."

Manager of the 1961 and 1962 World Champion Yankees, Ralph Houk: "I played with DiMaggio before I played and managed Mickey. Nobody, but nobody, could hit a ball as hard and as far from both sides of the plate as Mickey could. He was just awesome."

St. Louis Cardinals great shortstop and former National League MVP Marty Marion: "There's one thing he can't do very well. He can't throw left-handed. When he goes in for that, we'll have the perfect ballplayer."

Nellie Fox, who often fought with Hank Bauer and who was no Yankees fan: "On two legs, Mickey would have been the greatest ballplayer who ever lived."

Manager Harry Craft, who knew a great outfielder when he saw one and had been a fine defensive center fielder:" He can run, steal bases, throw, hit for average, and hit with power like I've never seen. Just don't put him at shortstop."

And of greatest significance, because being great is not enough for the greatest, who consider winning all that matters, Yankees' shortstop Tom Tresh: "We never thought we could lose as long as Mickey was playing. The point was, we had Mickey and the other team didn't."

When Mickey Mantle trotted out to his position in centerfield, there was an indefinable uniqueness about him. He possessed a style and grace that was his alone and is exhibited by the few who are special. Teammates, opponents, and fans felt his presence and incomparable talent. He was *Mickey Mantle*.

When Mantle stepped into the batter's box, there was an undercurrent of excitement on the field and in the stands. Ballplayers stopped what they were doing and watched him take batting practice. Vendors stopped selling hotdogs and fans stopped drinking their beers. All eyes, whether it was practice or the game was on the line, focused on Mickey Mantle.

Each time Mickey stepped to the plate, every fan in the "Big Ballpark in the South Bronx" wondered if this would be the time that a fair ball finally left the Stadium. That alone made him special, because no one else in the game had the potential to actually do it. And yet, in complete juxtaposition, no one would be surprised if he dragged a bunt down the first baseline and beat it out for a hit. That is what made Mickey so great. No one in the history of the game, and that reads "no one," combined power and speed like Mickey Charles Mantle.

Batting left-handed, Mantle was timed running from the batters' box to first base in 3.1 seconds, which is almost inconceivable. As the years have passed, the 3.1 seconds have become 3.5 seconds because broadcasters and fans found it inconceivable that the time actually could have been 3.1 seconds. In order for broadcasters to maintain credibility, the higher time is used.

Willie Mays was almost as fast as Mickey, but Willie was a better base runner. As Allen Barra wrote, Mays made more of his speed than Mantle did of his. Mantle had more speed although he used it only when his team needed it.

There is no doubt that Willie was the better fielder. His instincts on fly balls were second to none, and he got as good a jump on the ball as anyone who ever played the game. Mickey was originally a shortstop who was challenged by ground balls, so he became a center fielder. Mickey got a decent jump on the ball and had sure hands, but it was his unmatched speed that made him into a top outfielder since it allowed him to compensate for his mistakes before they became errors or hits.

Mickey made some outstanding catches. One of the most often famous is the play he made on October 8, 1956 when he robbed Gil Hodges of extra bases to preserve what was on the way to becoming the first perfect game in World Series history. I didn't see it because I was in school. When I arrived home, some of my friends and I were getting ready to play ball at the park when Nicky DeVito, out of breath from running and from excitement, told us that Don Larsen had just pitched a perfect game in the World Series. We already knew that the Yankees had won the game, but we had no idea it had been a perfect game.

On that beautiful, sunny day at Yankee Stadium, Brooklyn's Sal Maglie and the Yankees' Don Larsen exchanged goose eggs until Mickey touched Maglie for a solo home run with two outs in the bottom of the fourth inning. Moments later, leading off the Brooklyn fifth, Gil Hodges hit a blast to deep left center field that looked like a sure hit. Mickey raced as fast as he could toward the gap in left center field, stretched his body as far as possible, stuck out his left hand and Gil Hodges' attempt at a double died in Mickey's glove. It was called a "miraculous catch" by no less an expert than legendary *New York Times* baseball scribe John Drebinger. Despite my love for Mickey, I know that Willie made an even better play. It wasn't his catch in the 1954 World Series of a Vic Wertz bid for extra bases. It was probably the greatest outfield play ever.

It was August 15, 1951. The New York Giants, who trailed the Brooklyn Dodgers by 11 and one-half games, were in the midst of what would become a 16 game winning streak. The greatest rivals in baseball history were playing the second game of a crucial three game series at the Polo Grounds. The score was 1-1 in the top of the eighth inning.

Billy Cox, a fairly fast runner at that point in his career, was on third for Brooklyn, with pitcher Ralph Branca on first. There was only one out. Our friend Carl Furillo, one of baseball's most underrated players, was the batter, facing New York's big right-hander, Jim Hearn. The outfielders played Furillo to pull, with left fielder Monte Irvin shaded toward the left field line, right fielder Don Mueller playing well off the line in right and Willie Howard Mays Jr. moved over to left center field.

Hearn went into the stretch, checked the runners at first and third and delivered. Furillo hit a fly ball to right center field that, to all eyes, appeared would be deep enough to score Cox with the lead run. Mays broke to his left immediately. Running at full speed, he made the catch, a catch that other outstanding center fielders would have made, but Mays had to run towards the right field foul line to get to the ball, so he was moving away from home plate. If he stopped running to set himself for the throw home there would be no chance to throw out Cox tagging up from third.

Mays didn't break stride. He planted his left foot, made a complete whirling pivot on the dead run as if he were a discus thrower and uncorked a fantastic throw home. The ball came flying toward the plate. First baseman Whitey Lockman, the cutoff man, let the throw go through, which was a very wise decision. Giants' catcher Wes Westrum caught the ball belt high. He planted himself for a collision as he tagged out the sliding, incredulous Cox.

The crowd's initial reaction was shocking silence. No one believed what he saw. Then reality set in and there was a tremendous roar. Fans had seen one of the greatest plays of all time. It wasn't one of the greatest *catches* of all times. It was one of the greatest *plays* of all time. Many outfielders might have caught the ball, but few, if any them, could have caught the ball and then made the throw home Mays made to get the runner.

By the way, I really think that until he was hurt when Red Schoendienst fell on his shoulder in the 1957 World Series, Mickey really did have a better arm than Willie. Despite the fact that Willie made the greatest catch of all time and was a great hitter, Mickey was almost as great a defensive player and was a more effective hitter. Why?

Because Mickey was one of the greatest right-handed hitters of all time and Mickey was one of the greatest left-handed hitters of all time. He could hit the ball 500 feet from the right side. He could hit the ball just as far batting left-handed. Willie had to settle on being one of the greatest right-handed hitters of all time. Not bad, but not Mickey Mantle.

Shirley Povich, the outstanding baseball writer for the *Washington Post*, covered many of Mickey's games. One Povich article, written at the time that Mickey was dying, captures the essence of Mickey Mantle's greatness:

He could run. That was an anomaly. When did it ever happen, before Mantle, that the biggest hitter on any team, the guy who hit the farthest in the league, was also the fastest man on his team and its best bunter? Never.

A Mantle specialty was the drag bunt that let him break from the left side of the plate. The drag bunt is an art of the game and none captured it like Mickey. You lay it down to a spot that gives both the pitcher and the first baseman a fit. Who fields it? No matter. They wouldn't get Mickey, who was already surging toward the bag.

When did Mickey Mantle bunt? Whenever he felt like it. From Casey Stengel he had a blank check. Bunt when you feel like it. Drag bunting on the count of 3 and 2 when a foul tip would get you out was rejected as a tactic until Mantle made it one of his specialties. You could do it if you had Mickey's supreme ability to do it.

Could Mantle play the outfield? When Joe DiMaggio quit and Mickey over in center field there was no lowering of standards. What a compliment. Maybe he didn't quite have DiMag's arm, but he had more than Joe's speed. He, too, could outrun a fly ball.

For many years a thought has occurred to me. I covered Willie Mays's great catch of that steamer Vic Wertz hit in the 1954 World Series. Mays took one look at that zinger toward deepest center in the Polo Grounds, turned and caught up with the ball and speared it with his back to the plate, a wondrous catch. Who else could have made it? Mickey Mantle.

One had to have seen Mickey play to completely understand what it felt like for the fans when he stepped up to the plate. Remember Mark McGwire and Sammy Sosa in September of 1998? Remember when it was Pete Rose's turn to bat at the time he was tied for lifetime hits with Ty Cobb? Well, those were special occasions that happened a few times or only once in a lifetime. Every time Mickey Mantle stepped to the plate was a special occasion. It was an experience that was filled with the anticipation of seeing the longest home run ever hit, the fear of seeing Mickey getting injured, the apprehension of Mickey striking out.

All-time great Hall of Famer, the vastly underrated Al Kaline, recalled the time he was leaving Briggs Stadium in Detroit after a game against the Yankees. A young boy blurted out, "You're not half as good as Mickey Mantle." Kaline was taken aback at first but then responded, "Son, nobody is half as good as Mickey Mantle!"

CHAPTER 12

GREENIES, STEROIDS AND STATISTICS

Mickey Mantle was five-feet and 11 inches tall. He weighed 195 pounds, yet with the possible exception of Babe Ruth, no player in baseball history hit the ball farther more often or more dramatically. Mantle did not lift weights, nor did he work out at the gym. In the 1950s and 1960s, players, team owners, trainers, and many in the medical establishment believed that being too muscular would inhibit the flexibility players needed to be effective. Synthetic steroids were not used in professional sports, but in *Ball Four*, Jim Bouton confirmed what many knew but refused to acknowledge. A preponderance of baseball players used amphetamines, primarily to counteract the effects of a hangover or the fatigue of a long season.

Amphetamines are performance "enablers," while steroids are performance "enhancers." This is not a play on words. Amphetamines allow players to retain their abilities despite fatigue. They do not increase a player's abilities nor do they allow a player past his peak to regain skills eroded by time.

Called "greenies" because they are little green pills, amphetamines were first used by baseball players in the 1940s. They fight fatigue, mask pain, increase pulse rate and alertness, and decrease reaction time, but they cannot improve reaction time beyond that which an individual's genetics dictates. Amphetamines are addictive that increase the risk of heart attack or stroke.

During World War II, pilots and infantrymen received amphetamines to help them remain alert. The pills were legal and sold over the counter. Baseball players who served their country often were assigned to military baseball teams and were given amphetamines. When the war ended, they had a new helper.

One of baseball's great sluggers, Ralph Kiner, led or tied the National League in home runs seven consecutive seasons, starting in 1946. Kiner relates how, when he entered the Pittsburgh Pirates clubhouse for the first time after returning from the navy, he found amphetamines in the training room. One time, late in the season before the second game of a doubleheader, Kiner took some Benzedrine from one of the trainers.

"All the trainers in all the ballparks had them," Kiner said. "You needed to perform your best and you were going to use everything that's legal to help you do it. You worked to get that job and you wanted to stay in the lineup. If you got out of the lineup, you might never get back in."

Players used amphetamines even after they were declared a controlled substance in 1970, and their use has continued into the 21st century. After the United States regulated amphetamines, they remained over the counter drugs in Latin America, which has not changed. The winter leagues continue to expose players to easily accessible amphetamines and it is claimed that virtually every player who ever played in a Latin American county has experienced a greenie-loaded pot of coffee.

A player agent and a current coach interviewed on ESPN and speaking independently, claimed that stimulants are pervasive in today's game. "In the old days, a player might pop one to get up for a day game after a night game. Now guys use them more and more. They're passed out like candy in the clubhouse." Baseball now tests players for amphetamine use.

If Mickey used amphetamines, and Jim Bouton claims that he did, it brings us back to performance "enhancers" versus performance "enablers." Greenies might have helped Mickey play at his level of ability but they did not increase that ability.

During the last 25 years, there has been a fitness revolution. Remember when Jack LaLanne was the only game in town and people were embarrassed to jog in the city? Mickey was not one for exercise. I remember his remarking about how difficult spring training was because he got "soft" during the off-season although it usually didn't take Mickey too long to get back into shape. A comment he made, in an off-handed manner when we were at dinner after shooting *The 500 Home Run Club*, flashes into my mind occasionally during the baseball season. "You know Tom, Dr. Gaynor (Yankees' team physician) and Gus Mauch or Joe Soares would give me exercises to do after an injury, but sometimes my bad knee wouldn't let me do them." Even when Mickey had to exercise, he couldn't.

Roger Clemens and Barry Bonds are known for their arduous, demanding exercise regimens, among other things. When Clemens was a rookie, he was much smaller and thinner than during the last few years of his career. Bonds was so lanky and thin that he often batted leadoff his first couple of seasons with the Pirates, not that being thin and lanky is a requirement of being a leadoff hitter. Clemens has been called one of the greatest pitchers of all time. Among hitters, Barry has been ranked just below Babe Ruth. Both credit their late-career super seasons to their rigorous workouts. I don't think so and either does 2016 society.

It is doubtful if exercise would have helped Mickey much with respect to his strength because his muscles, as Dr. Gaynor said, were too strong for his body. He might have hurt himself even if he had worked out, but exercise would have helped him aerobically and probably would have helped him stay in top-notch shape longer. Maybe working out could have helped to prevent some of his pulled hamstrings. Of course, we always return to the bad knees, which nothing could have helped.

Volumes have been written about what Mickey would have accomplished if he had been healthy. To get an idea, let us assume that in his partial seasons, he had played the entire season. Baseball-Reference.com projects every player's average 162 game season. These are Mickey's results:

AB	547
R	113
H	163
2B	23
3B	5
HR	36
RBI	102
SB	10
CS	3
BB	117
SO	115
BA	0.298
DP	8

Since Mickey played 18 seasons and he averaged 36 home runs a season, he would have hit well over 600 home runs with almost 3,000 hits.

Now that the easy part is done, we can broach a controversial topic. I mentioned earlier that in our conversations, Mickey adamantly opposed drug use. When we first met, I had to overcome the first impression produced by my long hair, beard, and involvement with the music world, which Mickey easily could have interpreted as the appearance of one who was familiar with pot. When he learned that my first love was country music, his suspicions were softened.

Some fascinating comparisons can be made regarding performance enhancing drugs.

After the 1994 strike, offense increased dramatically. From 1995 -2007, teams averaged 4.84 runs a game. During Mickey Mantle's career, teams averaged 4.23 runs a game. There is a statistical tool called Analysis of Variance, which is used to discover if the difference between two sets of data is caused by chance. For example, Mickey averaged 36 home runs over a 162-game season. Billy Martin averaged 10 home runs over a 162-game season. The difference between Mickey's and Billy's totals is not due to chance.

An analysis of variance comparing the average runs scored between 1995 - 2007 and 1951 - 1968 reveals that a statistically significant difference exists at the 0.0001 level, which means that there is 1 in 10,000 chance that the difference is due to chance. Analysis of variance cannot attribute a cause.

RUNS/GAME: 1994-2007 v. 1951-1968

YEAR	AL R/G	NL R/G
2007	4.90	4.71
2006	4.97	4.76
2005	4.76	4.45
2004	5.01	4.64
2003	4.86	4.61
2002	4.81	4.45
2001	4.86	4.70
2000	5.30	5.00
1999	5.18	5.00
1998	5.01	4.60
1997	4.93	4.60

1996	5.39	4.68
1995	5.06	4.63
AVR		
RUNS	5.00	4.68

YEAR	AL R/G	NL R/G
1951	4.63	4.46
1952	4.18	4.17
1953	4.46	4.75
1954	4.19	4.56
1955	4.44	4.53
1956	4.66	4.25
1957	4.23	4.38
1958	4.17	4.40
1959	4.36	4.40
1960	4.39	4.24
1961	4.53	4.52
1962	4.44	4.48
1963	4.08	3.81
1964	4.06	4.01
1965	3.94	4.03
1966	3.89	4.09
1967	3.70	3.84
1968	3.41	3.43
AVR		
RUNS	4.21	4.24

Whether teams score more runs (post 1994) because of the smaller ballparks, a livelier baseball, a smaller strike zone, a lower pitching mound, better hitters, worse pitchers or a combination of some or all of these factors is not known. What is known is that the increased run production is due to chance. There aren't too many folks who think when Luis Gonzalez hit 57 home runs in 2001 he was a better home run hitter than Mickey Mantle.

Mickey really wasn't too concerned about statistics. I mentioned earlier how he thought that he hit .357 in 1957 and I reluctantly said that he batted

.365. Mickey admired Ralph Houk, yet sometimes doing what seems best may produce unwanted consequences. Ralph Houk was indirectly responsible for Mickey losing his .300 career average.

The month was January, the year was 1966, and the decision was that Mickey Mantle was going to retire.

Mickey was coming off the worst season of his career. He batted .255 with only 19 home runs and 46 RBIs in 122 games. A revealing statistic is that while Mickey appeared in 122 games, he completed only 36 of them. At the age of 34, repeated injuries had finally destroyed the player who had been a faster runner.

Houk was perceptive when he explained why Mantle shouldn't retire after his dismal 1965 season. "...no one would want him to go out that way, but that he didn't realize what he meant to the public, the Yankees, and his fellow players. Just having Mickey Mantle on the team has been a great influence on all of us. And I told him he didn't realize how good he was."

Houk told Mickey that he didn't have to play every day. Manager Johnny Keane would pick his spots, not playing Mickey in second games of double headers and resting him when there was a day game after a night game. Mickey bought it.

After the 1965 season, Mickey's lifetime batting average was .306, his on base average was .426, and his slugging average was .576. He had hit 473 home runs and had 145 stolen bases in 179 attempts for a remarkable .810 average. I've often wondered where Mickey would rank if he hadn't listened to Ralph Houk and had retired after the 1965 season.

Despite no longer being Mickey Mantle, there were still some good days in 1965. On June 22, the Yankees were in seventh place with a record of 29-35, trailing the first place Minnesota Twins by 10 and a half games.

In the first game of a doubleheader at the real, genuine Yankee Stadium against their cousins from Kansas City, the Athletics, 13,129 fans paid their way in with the hope that their team would get started. The Yankees dropped the opener, 6-2, despite a Mickey Mantle home run. In the nightcap, with the A's leading 2-0, Mickey led off the fourth inning with a walk and went to second when Tommy Tresh was safe on shortstop Bert Campaneris' error. After Ellie Howard flied out to right, Kansas City right-hander Fred Talbot made a wild pitch. Mickey, hustling too much, tried to score from second and was thrown out at the plate, but that was not what hurt the Yankees.

Mickey pulled a muscle in his left leg, which team physician Dr. Sydney

120

Gaynor thought was just a strain. But this was Mickey Mantle and it turned out that the injury was a pulled hamstring muscle.

By the middle of July, it was apparent that the Yankees were not going to win the pennant. They had to rebuild and many in the media felt that Mickey might never again have a Mickey Mantle type season because he had been too banged up for too long. The problem was a Catch-22 because the injured legs prevented Mickey from exercising in such ways that would prevent future injuries. It was thought that he would play two or three more years, but that anything he contributed would be a bonus. The Yankees had to rebuild as if he were not on the roster.

On September 2, in Anaheim, he drove in four runs with a home run and single as Whitey Ford went the distance in beating Marcellino Lopez, 8 - 1. Bobby Richardson led off the game with a single and Tommy Tresh doubled him to third, bringing up left fielder Mickey Mantle. There was no thought of intentionally walking Mantle, who made the Angels pay when he hit a 400-foot home run. Briefly, it was like the old days of Mantle and Ford.

The 1952 World Series illustrates how statistics can be meaningless. Billy saved the Series when he made his famous lunging catch of a Jackie Robinson pop up with the bases loaded and two outs. When Robinson hit the ball, it seemed as if the inning would end with either first baseman Joe Collins, third baseman Gil McDougald, or even pitcher Bob Kuzava making the play. None did. The ball got caught in the wind, and it seemed, for a fleeting moment, that the only thing on the field that could catch the ball was the wind. Collins seemed to lose sight of the pop up. Kuzava and McDougald were frozen at their positions.

The ball completed the first half of its parabolic arc and was on its way down. Three Brooklyns, as Red Barber would say, were racing around the bases with the runs that would give them the lead. Suddenly, on the television, the voice of Mel Allen screamed out, "Here comes Billy Martin. The ball is falling fast. And Martin makes a knee high, lunging catch to save three runs." How about that?

Billy Martin didn't have the gaudy statistics of a star, but he had a fierce desire to win at any cost, which is something that numbers cannot measure. Frank Lane, succinctly described Billy Martin's value when he stated simply that, "He's the kind of guy you'd like to kill if he's playing for the other team, but you'd like 10 of him on your side."

CHAPTER 13

THE DEVIL WENT DOWN TO GEORGIA ... AND THE BRONX

Early in my career I had put together a promotion with entertainer Charlie Daniels. Charlie had a monster hit, "The Devil Went Down to Georgia," that propelled the Charlie Daniels Band to both a Grammy and a role in the hugely successful *Urban Cowboy* film with John Travolta.

Charlie's background was a tapestry of American music and culture. He had written a hit song for Elvis, *It Hurts Me*, and had recorded the *Nashville Skyline, New Morning, and Self Portrait* albums with Bob Dylan, who was a great admirer of Charlie's musical skills. In Dylan's 2004 autobiography, *Chronicles*, he comments on Charlie:

"I was wondering who he (record producer Bob Johnston) was going to bring to the sessions this time and was hoping he'd bring Charlie Daniels .... I felt I had a lot in common with Charlie. The kind of phrases he'd use, his sense of humor, his relationship to work, his tolerance for certain things. Felt we had dreamed the same dream with all the same distant places. A lot of his recollections seemed to coincide with mine. Charlie would fiddle with stuff and make sense of it. I had no band at the time and relied on the A & R (artist and repertoire) man or producer to throw one together. When Charlie was around, something good would usually come out of the sessions.

"I felt our early histories were somewhat similar. Charlie eventually struck it big. After hearing the Allman Brothers and the side-winding Lynyrd Skynyrd, he'd find his groove and prove himself with his own brand of dynamics, coming up with a new form of hillbilly boogie that was pure genius."

In 1976, Charlie performed numerous concerts for Jimmy Carter, who credited Charlie with keeping his presidential campaign afloat financially. Also, Charlie was best friends with the western writer, Louis L'Amour, who arguably sold more books than any American writer. Kathy L'Amour chose Charlie to do the eulogy at, as Charlie called him, "Mr. L'Amour's," funeral in 1988. Charlie also did the eulogy for Lynyrd Skynyrd lead singer, Ronnie Van Zant.

Charlie and I became close friends over the years. I was his liaison to corporate America and had developed a good sense of how each entity needed to communicate with the other. I remember a very Senior Executive at my company coming up to Charlie and gushing, "*Billy* Daniels, I'm one of your biggest fans." Obviously.

Charlie and I hit it off immediately. A strong bond developed when we discussed how important our grandfathers were in our lives. I think my best memory was surprising Charlie in Holland while I was on a business trip and he was touring Europe. It was during the time period when the fad created by *Urban Cowboy* was at its peak.

Charlie, the members of his band and I decided to go to a western club in Amsterdam. As we entered, the house band was playing Charlie's multi-million selling hit, "The Devil Went Down to Georgia." Imagine the look on the faces of the house band and club patrons when, as Charlie Daniels' signature hit is being performed, in walks Charlie Daniels with his band. Of course, Charlie was coerced into getting on the stage, but he didn't need much coercion. He did a rebel-rousing version of Chuck Berry's *Johnny B. Goode*, sending the room into a frenzy.

Now, boys will be boys and Johnny won't always be good. The evening ended with an altercation between some rowdies in the crowd and Charlie's road crew. "Skinny," a member of Charlie's group, was a former football player at the University of Tennessee. Built like a bulldozer, he put three rowdy Dutchman out of commission. The rest of the potential combatants, using their better judgment, backed off. Oh, what a night.

To this day, Charlie Daniels is one of my dearest friends. I have enormous respect for the way he lives his life. Once I overheard him refer to me as a "good 'un," which is redneck, southern hillbilly for a good, trusted friend. Quite a compliment for this Bronx-born Italian from a "redneck."

Charlie was involved with the *500 Home Run Club* video, which had great momentum going for it. One afternoon, during a brainstorming session, we decided to do a major Charlie Daniel's Band concert at Mickey's House in the Bronx—Yankee Stadium. Charlie had a huge New York following, especially on Long Island, where all the Southern rock bands were revered. He was a big baseball fan who often sang the National Anthem at major league stadiums. Why not have Mickey introduce the Band the day of the concert? Charlie quickly agreed, and not surprisingly, Mickey loved the idea. "Hell, I'll bring along Billy (Martin), and we'll have a hoot."

We worked out our deal with the Yankees for the concert date to be in August 1989. They would sell the *500 Home Run Club* video at Yankee Stadium and put an ad on every Yankees' game ticket for one year. Prior to the concert, we produced a television commercial to publicize the video in which my son, Luke would return to the scene of his crime, the field at Yankee Stadium. Luke would hand Charlie his fiddle and Charlie would take an imaginary swing, using the instrument as a baseball bat. Several of the Yankees stopped by for the 10:00 AM shoot. Charlie was charged up about the concert and meeting Mickey. He understood that Yankee Stadium was historic, almost sacred turf.

The day of the concert arrived. There was no rain. There was just blue sky with packed stands on a Sunday afternoon. The Yankees would play their regularly scheduled game after which Charlie would go on 30 minutes after the game ended.

My wife, children and granddaughters are the best parts of my life. But walking on the field and basically being in charge of what was about to happen was a once-in-a-lifetime thrill. I gazed up to the luxury boxes, which had been provided for me, and saw my Mom, beaming with pride, accompanied by various family members, including my sister Maria and husband Bob, and customers of *Cabin Fever Entertainment*.

The plan was quite simple. A large *Cabin Fever Entertainment* SUV, which held Charlie, his musicians, most of whom were from the deep south, and a Yankees' executive, was parked on a South Bronx street, beneath the overhead train tracks. A gate would be opened allowing the Charlie Daniels Band to be driven through the Yankees' bullpen to centerfield, where a huge stage had been constructed in centerfield, facing home plate.

In those days, the South Bronx was a dangerous place. As Charlie and the crew waited in the van, three men wearing blood stained garments started banging on the windows of the truck.

"Who are they?" "Lock the doors!" came the pleas from the band members. The only calm occupant was my brother Ed, who was driving the truck. "Don't freak out!" he said. "It's only the Losenski brothers, I know them."

Ed rolled down his window and gave each of them a backstage pass to the concert. The Losenskis were butchers who worked in a slaughterhouse. They were running late, coming from Connecticut to the Bronx, and hadn't bothered changing clothes. My brother had told them to "meet me under the "El" train platform in right field." To everyone's relief, the truck left the mean streets of the South Bronx and rolled onto the plush grass and track of Yankee Stadium.

I greeted Charlie when the truck arrived at home plate then went to get Mickey, who had just arrived in the runway leading to the dugout. As I walked across the field, somebody called my attention to the huge scoreboard above the centerfield bleachers.

"The Yankees wish to thank Tom Molito and *Cabin Fever Entertainment* for today's event."

I thought back to the conversation I had with the elderly Italian immigrant construction worker who said to me, "You went to college? You don't have to do this? You are really stupid!" Seeing my name in 12-foot letters on the scoreboard gave me a sense of satisfaction and accomplishment.

I met Mickey, who was attired in his best western wear and cowboy hat, and noticed that he looked relaxed. I do remember that he made certain to greet all the ground crew workers. Mickey even remembered the names of those who had been there during his playing days. It struck me as typical Mickey Mantle to go out of his way for the working folk.

Charlie and Mickey initiated a friendship that afternoon, and I believe the foundation was their working class backgrounds. Charlie's family worked in the tobacco fields and lumber industry around Wilmington, North Carolina. Mickey's family, of course, worked in the zinc mines of Oklahoma. Over the years, I watched both men relate to all sorts of people, but both seemed most comfortable around working-class people. Both Charlie and Mickey were extremely humble. Charlie referred to himself as just a "fat boy playing the fiddle," while Mickey saw himself as just a baseball player who never understood the deity status thrust upon him. Large egos do not increase greatness.

The crowd spotted Mickey as a low murmur quickly grew into loud cheers. Mickey's appearance had been a well-kept secret and the fans were ecstatic. I shouted to Charlie over the roar of the crowd, who 30 seconds after spotting Mickey saw Charlie emerge from the *Cabin Fever Entertainment* SUV. I introduced them. "Charlie, meet Mickey Mantle," as if he didn't know.

The stage could only be reached by climbing a set of stairs specially constructed for the concert. I saw a problem. I positioned myself next to Mickey to give him something to brace himself against. Little did he know, I was so nervous that I too needed bracing.

Mickey and Charlie hugged each other, which produced an instant rapport. "Billy Martin is here somewhere," Mickey said to Charlie before he started addressing the crowd. "You all are in for a good down-home time. These old boys are from Mt. Juliet, Tennessee ... Charlie Daniels, welcome to Yankee Stadium."

As Charlie kicked off the concert with his super patriotic song *In America*, which was a reaction to the Iran hostage crisis describing a united America, Mickey and I made our way to one of the luxury boxes. As we arrived in the suite, somebody pulled me aside to fill me in on Billy Martin's whereabouts. Billy had appeared at the suite's entrance in his best Wyatt Earp outfit that included a black hat, a big silver buckle, a western string tie and silver trimmed boots with spurs! He was anxious to get into the suite, hear Charlie and have something to eat and maybe a drink or two.

One problem, a major problem, was that Yankee Stadium security had been instructed not to let Billy around any location in the Stadium that served liquor. George Steinbrenner was now treating Billy like a man with a problem, as opposed to simply a volatile manager. Naturally, Billy's temper surfaced when he was prevented from getting a drink.

Mickey and Greer soon were mingling with all the corporate high-level Executives and *Cabin Fever Entertainment* customers. Upon meeting John Bucchigiano, the UST Chief Financial Officer who wrote the checks for *Cabin Fever Entertainment*, Mickey requested "his autograph" while giving him a hug. It was a funny scene. This was a complete role reversal. Mickey was requesting an autograph, which beautifully illustrated Mickey's sense of dry humor.

Charlie came up to the suite after the concert as he and Mickey identified their many mutual friends. They agreed to keep in touch and play a round of golf in Dallas. A few days later, a large package arrived at the Regency Hotel for Mickey. It was a huge black cowboy hat. Charlie had sent it as a "thank you" to Mickey, who delighted in wearing it on Park Avenue, with his ears sticking out. Greer was mortified, which, naturally, made Mickey love it even more. Charlie and Mickey stayed friends right up until Mickey's passing.

In 2004, Charlie commented in the book, *Our Mickey*, about the events of the day: "In August 1989, I was doing a gig at Yankee Stadium. Mickey came to the concert unannounced and incognito with a huge bull rider's hat pulled way down to his ears. He looked like the village idiot. After the show, he came backstage and instead of hobnobbing with the other celebrities, he insisted on shaking hands with every member of my road crew and musicians."

Yet another example of how down to earth Mickey Mantle was. He never forgot his roots, his values, or his humanity. He never waved a fist in the air after hitting a home run. No, after hitting a home run, Mickey Mantle circled the bases as quickly as possible, with his head down, trying not to make the pitcher who gave up the home run feel any worse than he already felt.

CHAPTER 14

THE INNER CIRCLE

A few days after the concert at Yankee Stadium, I celebrated my 45th birthday. Luke had made me a birthday card that contained several drawings of my favorite things, such as pizza, country music, fishing, and, of course, baseball. He signed the card, "Love, Mickey Luke Molito," knowing the spot in my heart for Mickey. He also did a drawing of Mickey with the big Number 7 prominently displayed. I thought it was cute and that Mickey would get a kick out of seeing it. I mailed the card to the Regency Hotel. Mickey's reaction was not what I expected.

A few days after sending the card, Kathleen and I returned home from dinner at a local pub. We were told by our daughter, Christine, who was babysitting Laura, that Mickey Mantle had called and he seemed "sad." It wasn't very late on a Saturday evening, so I returned the call. Mickey picked up.

"I got your card, I didn't know you named your son after me!" Naming children after Mickey was very common not only with his fans, but also with his teammates on the Yankees. Before I could explain Luke's sense of humor, Mickey started weeping! "I never told my father I loved him and I never got a card like this." I did my best to assure Mickey that we lived in different eras and that I was sure his Dad knew Mickey loved him. He seemed so vulnerable that night. At that moment, he wasn't Mickey Mantle, the baseball superstar. He was Mickey Mantle, a son and a father.

After talking to Mickey, I reflected on how fragile Mickey was, both as a person and as a baseball player. Maybe that created some of the devotion and loyalty from his fans. I'd been interviewed by the *Sports Card Trader* magazine for our video and had compared Mickey to another legend. "He's not unlike

Hector, the greatest Trojan Warrior in Greek Mythology." I continued, "Hector was a flawed warrior. He took an arrow in his heel, his Achilles heel."

My analogy was that as great as Mickey was as a ball player, there is the unknown quality of how great he could have been if he had remained healthy. During his career, magazines and newspapers carried photographs of Mickey and his taped legs. Before every game, he spent more than forty-five minutes taping himself up. Teammates marveled at how, with the tape extended from his buttocks to his ankles, he went onto the field, beat out a bunt, stole a base, hit a tape measure home run, or made a great catch. Those who have never experienced what Mickey went through which includes most of us, could ever truly comprehend Mickey's courage.

Ballplayers knew what a Mickey Mantle with good legs could have achieved. Clete Boyer, who witnessed the 1961 home run race as the Yankees' third baseman and later played for the Braves, was once asked if he thought Mickey would have hit 60 home runs playing in a smaller stadium like Atlanta. "No" was Boyer's reply, "He would have hit eighty!"

Left-handed pitcher Leo "Bud" Daley said that, "There was an unwritten rule on the club that Mickey didn't steal unless the score was tied or it was a one run game. Mickey could have stolen 100 bases a year if his legs had been sound."

Tony Kubek wrote in his book, *Sixty-One*, that by 1961, Mickey's legs were so bad that it wasn't unusual for him to need help getting out of a cab. "He'd sort of brace himself and put out his hand. One of us would grab him by the wrist and literally pull him out of the cab." Mickey was a physical anomaly. Yankees' team physician Dr. Sidney Gaynor compared Mickey's muscles to Popeye's. His muscles were too strong for his joints. Dr. Gaynor commented that Mickey's joints -- his wrists, knees, and ankles -- were extremely frail but that his muscles were as strong as any Dr. Gaynor had ever seen. Mickey's muscles were simply too strong for his bones and the muscles tore apart Mickey's tendons and ligaments.

The children of the 1950s and 1960s did more than follow Mickey's statistics. Mickey Mantle was an integral part of our lives that was ever present in almost everything we did. We could be in class, on a date, watching a movie, or doing almost anything when Mickey Mantle would come to mind. His presence was always felt. Comedian Billy Crystal was quoted as saying, "Mickey Mantle was my childhood." We "felt" his pain.

I recently met an old friend who told me a story about his childhood fears. When he went to bed at night he worried about his parents, but also tossed and turned over his concern for Mickey. Today, he has a cat named Mickey Mantle. My friend was not unique.

We all worried about Mickey Mantle. Would he be able to play today? How long would his latest injury keep him sidelined? How long would his career last with such bad legs?

I actually met several members of Mickey's family after Mickey's passing. It helped me understand Mickey's reaction to my son's birthday card and the complexities of his family life. I met with David and Danny Mantle in the late 1990s. I had developed an outline for a possible film called *1951* and wanted the Mantle family involved. My concept was to take a two-year period of Mickey's life, from the ages of 19 to 20, illustrate the incredible pressure he was under, and dramatize how it forged the man he was to become, both positively and negatively. We created an outline of that two-year period:

The media projects the still-developing Mantle as better than Ruth and DiMaggio.

He moves from rural America to the heart of New York City.

He is inflicted with a serious knee injury.

He's sent back to the minor leagues.

He's taken advantage of by unscrupulous New York businessmen.

His shyness is interpreted as rudeness by both media and Yankee fans.

He is classified as 4F and ineligible for the Korean War. As he fails on the field he is taunted as a draft dodger.

He is indoctrinated to the pleasures of New York City by a slick New Yorker from Queens and a street fighter from Oakland -- Whitey Ford and Billy Martin.

His father dies. He marries Merlyn Johnson.

The Mantle boys liked the project, but for various reasons, it was never produced. I was in competition with *61**, a fine film produced for HBO by Billy Crystal. But while discussing the project, I forged a relationship with Danny and David.

Mickey had four sons -- Mickey Jr., Danny, David and Billy. Sadly, Mickey Jr. and Billy died young, succumbing to the cruel Mantle family history of early death. Danny handled business for the surviving Mantle sons. David is almost a twin of Mickey, and although David could be serious, he inherited his father's sense of humor as well as his love of partying all night. When he called me, he disguised his voice and told me that it was the police, the FBI, or the IRS.

Both Danny and David were drinking buddies with their dad. The three of them cherished those moments despite the pitfalls of depending on alcohol. Danny actually had talked Mickey into entering rehab at the Betty Ford Treatment Center, where Mickey received more cards and letters than anyone who had ever attended the facility. Significantly, it was the first time that Mickey realized how much he meant to everyone. He was beginning to realize that he was really loved.

Like his father, David enjoyed southern rock music and I became his ticket contact for Charlie Daniels and his favorite band, Lynryd Skynyrd. David had a special pinstriped motorcycle with a painting highlighting his Dad's career. One night he showed up at a Lynryd Skynyrd concert in Atlanta, wearing his biker outfit, complete with a Confederate flag bandana on his head. I stood next to him for half of the show before realizing it was David. He was a big guy who was very intimidating. I deliberately had avoided eye contact before realizing it was David.

After Mickey's passing, a national magazine ran a long article on the complexities of his family life and spelled out that parenting was not one of Mickey's greatest skills. Merlyn Mantle had done the bulk of parenting

I met Merlyn Mantle once after Mickey's death. *Cabin Fever Entertainment* had donated money to Mickey's foundation for organ donors. A photograph of Merlyn was taken alongside the plaque in front of Mickey's restaurant. I had expected an elderly woman, but was surprised by the pretty, petite blonde in a black leather jacket. We had a cup of coffee and Merlyn discussed overcoming her own drinking problems. She grew misty-eyed several times discussing Mickey as I sensed that she was still very much in love with her high school sweetheart. I remember her saying; "I loved him before he became Mickey Mantle."

Reflecting back, I was very fortunate. I recently read in a book by Mickey Herskowitz, a frequent Mantle biographer, that only Mickey's inner circle knew that Mickey really didn't live with his family the last decade of his life. Herskowitz went on to say that those who became his "new best friend" turned off Mickey. Additionally, if you called too often or hung around when not invited, your "inner circle" status would soon be taken away. I was always extremely aware of these parameters.

Greer and Mickey had a special relationship whose love was obvious when I was around them. At the end of his life, Mickey was reunited with his family and a deep loving bond was experienced.

We still exchange Christmas cards with Greer, who has moved on with her life and seems very happy.

CHAPTER 15

MICKEY MANTLE ALMOST SLEPT HERE

As my family and my job demands grew, the early 1990s became more and more hectic. We had moved to a special house in Bedford, New York. Where else would the founder of *Cabin Fever Entertainment* live but in a log cabin. Fittingly, my favorite toy as a kid had been Lincoln logs.

The house had been custom built for Robert Halmi Jr., a prolific television producer. In the process of buying the house, Halmi and I became friends and did business together. Our biggest deal was *Cabin Fever Entertainment's* acquisition of the video rights to *Lonesome Dove*, the mini-series based on Larry McMurtry's Pulitzer Prize winning novel. *Cabin Fever Entertainment* sold a record number of videos for a television mini-series, which made *Cabin Fever Entertainment* a "player" in the entertainment business. To this day, *Lonesome Dove* has a cult status and a legion of fans. Robert Duvall says *Lonesome Dove* is his favorite on-screen role. "It is my *Hamlet*," he has said more than once.

Greer and Mickey knew we lived in a log house and wanted to come to see it. We had two horses, a Miniature and an Appaloosa with beautiful brown-and-white markings. Mickey asked if I rode. I sheepishly told him, "No, I just like watching them." Coming from Oklahoma, Mickey probably thought that "watching" horses was something that only a New Yorker would do.

Plans were set for Mickey and Greer to come up for a weekend visit. I mentioned the visit to my siblings and an unbelievable concoction of excuses was offered as a possible reason to drop by. Mickey and Greer referred to those who wanted to meet Mickey as "eyeballers." It would have obviously damaged our relationship with Mickey and Greer to have a passing parade of family and friends. We politely told all to stay away.

To my great disappointment, Mickey backed out of coming, but Greer visited with her delightful friend from North Carolina, Sandy Small. It was nice for Kathleen to be alone with Greer, since Mickey's presence usually dominated any situation and all topics revolved around him, which was fine with me, of course, but I am member of the cult.

Our cabin was pretty far back into the woods, high on a hill off the road. The guest room provided a view into the woods that was home to an array of wildlife that included deer, turkey, coyotes, foxes and rabbits, all involved with their daily activities. We added to the animal population by having a rooster, two goats, two dogs, a hamster, two cats and our horses. Greer told us that we would never get Mickey to sleep over if we didn't put curtains and blinds on the guestroom. It became a standard joke with both Mickey and Greer, "Got the curtains up yet?"

Over dinner, Greer told us a great Mickey Mantle story. While visiting Billy and Jill Martin in Binghamton, New York, Greer and Mickey decided to go to the Baseball Hall of Fame, which was a short distance away. When Mickey had been there for his induction in 1974, he didn't have much time to actually walk around the museum and discover more about some of *his* heroes. He was also anxious to see his plaque hanging in the hallowed hall, but Mickey was apprehensive that the "eyeballers" would recognize him and turn their visit into an autograph/photo session.

Greer told us that Mickey appeared in their rented car in the Martins' driveway wearing sunglasses, a large baseball cap (not Yankees) pulled low over his sunglasses and a windbreaker with a large collar up around his always-famous features. When they reached the Hall of Fame, Mickey walked around the building for 30 minutes. No one recognized him or paid any attention to him. Much to Greer's surprise, Mickey started speaking in a louder than normal voice.

"Look, Greer they have my bat that I hit that home run off Chuck Stobbs in Washington." Soon after, in a louder voice, "They have my Number 7 uniform that was retired on Mickey Mantle Day!"

None of these tactics worked. Greer had a really great ride back to Binghamton with a sheepish, embarrassed Mickey next to her, as she laughed all the way home. Sometimes, ego affects even the most humble of men.

Greer also touched on Mickey's drinking as well as our failed attempt to intervene via the Waldorf video of his speech. In the 2002 book, *Mickey Mantle: America's Prodigal Son*, Greer recalled how, "If we were at a place where I knew the bartenders, I'd talk to them and tell them to make his drinks real light. Then he got wise to that. I'd also fake headaches, and tell him I needed to go home."

Kathleen and I recalled how Greer complimented Mickey after dinner one night for not drinking too much. Considering he had a bottle of red wine and several vodka-and-tonics, the comment was revealing. I loved being with Mickey, but his drinking made him so vulnerable. When he was drinking, the conversations tended toward reassuring him and trying to make him feel less negative about his career, family life, childhood and business sense.

I do not drink if I can help it, but one night, I fell victim. It was either Billy Martin's or Mickey's birthday. I found myself in a limousine, riding around Manhattan, hitting numerous bars. I have no recollection except being in the backseat with Mickey and Billy.

The night passed quickly and somehow, some way, somebody deposited me at my office. I had an 8:00 A.M. meeting! The first person to greet me was Denise, my secretary. "What the hell happened to you?" she asked. Denise still laughs at the liquor on my breath and the disheveled and wrinkled suit and tie over my shoulder.

Even though Mickey never got to my house, he was ever present. I had collected Mantle memorabilia my whole life. I saved all the photos that decorated my childhood bedroom and simply added items. We had a small, unused room in the log house that was named "the shrine." The room was completely filled with scrapbooks, bats, balls, books, and memories. It wasn't close to Barry Halper's collections, but it was mine. One day, I inventoried the contents of the room.

Danbury Mint - ceramic Yankee Stadium (both pre 1973 and post 1973)
Yankee Stadium in "snow" globe
Metal Yankee Stadium music box
Cutout plastic stand-up of Mantle
Bronze Mantle coin – certificate of authenticity (2 different)
Mantle bobble head doll
Three scrap books; hundreds of photos, mementos, some autographed
Four ball caps – Mantle related

New York Times Commemorative Newspapers - Mantle, Ruth, Gehrig, DiMaggio
500th Home Run Poster
Mantle monument poster
Embossed Mantle collector card set - metallic from upper deck
Eight buttons/pins – various Mantle Home Runs
Audiotape - 60 Mantle Home Runs
Mantle action flip motion cards - 2 scenes
Mantle mug
Mantle three-dimensional scene
Mantle tie
Mantle 12' figure from Cooperstown collection
Two Mantle Tie-shirts, one Mantle Jersey from Restaurant (blue #7)
Mantle comic book – 1st edition
Twenty-five Magazines - Mantle on cover
Twenty-five original newspapers – Hall of fame, death, etc.
Four Mantle calendars
Three Mantle numbered registered ceramic plates
Numerous Mantle posters - some autographed
Mantle – NY Baseball insert from NY Times
Bag from Mickey Mantle Restaurant
Original signed contract to produce "500 Home Run Club" Video
Thirty framed photo's many autographed- some poster size
Twenty-five Mantle Video's plus bonus unused footage from production
Number 7 1952 replica jersey
Maris/Mantle autographed on same photo
Several X-rated notes from Mantle
More than 50 hard Mickey Mantle hard-covered books
One Reno Bertoia autographed photograph obtained in 1998.

Had Mickey come to Bedford, I'm not sure what I would have done with the shrine. I would have loved to know if he would have been curious about a Reno Bertoia autographed photo mixed in among my Mickey memorabilia. On one level he might have found my collection interesting, although I would also have risked becoming an "eyeballer" to Mickey.

When Greer had visited us, she took the collection in stride and expressed interest in some items she had never seen. Some dealers have

136

advised me to take advantage of Mickey's popularity in the memorabilia market, which would mean selling some of my collection, which is ridiculous. The collection is a link to my childhood as well as to Mickey. It is priceless in my opinion. And what collector of Mantle memorabilia tops off his collection with a Reno Bertoia autographed picture?

After I left the corporate world and our kids started marrying or moving out, Kathleen and I "downsized" to a smaller house. There was no longer space for a Mantle shrine, so Kathleen suggested a "Mickey bathroom." The room came out great, featuring many autographed poster sized photos in addition to some of Mickey's X-rated notes on $20 bills.

I've had many reactions to the room. Some individuals have thought it was strange; others warned me of someone walking off with an item or two. The best reaction was from a Yankee fan of my daughter, Laura, who exclaimed that it was the best room he had ever seen. He wanted to bring a cot to sleep in it.

As a footnote to my shrine, I also have some personal newspaper clippings and trophies from my own "baseball career." Ironically, my best year, like Mickey's, was 1956. I hit .453 with a league leading six homers in the Yonkers, New York, Little League.

We played our games on Welty Field, which like most fields in Yonkers, had no grass. Some of my homers were hard ground balls that rolled past the outfielders on the concrete-like field. Some were good shots that would have cleared the fence, if there had been one. I would have loved to limp around the bases like Mickey. It was amazing how everyone wanted Number 7 and how many 12 year-olds limped!

I never got to be Number 7 in youth baseball for a simple reason. I was the 41st toughest kid in my predominately Italian neighborhood. Oh, I was big and strong, but unlike most of the other kids, I didn't know how to fight. I also wasn't "crazy," which meant that I understand that sometimes, discretion is the better part of valor. In some ways, that was good because many of the kids were "regulars" at the local precinct and courthouse. One of the tougher kids on our team took Number 7, so I "had to wear" number four. I've heard that the Yankees' number four was a pretty good player.

I had a great thrill several years ago when my son, Luke, played at Fleming Park, one of my old Yonkers fields. He was playing in an adult league with players in their mid-20s who had some college or pro experience. To watch my son play on the same field that I had played on 40 years earlier was not only fun -- it was emotional. To top it off, Luke made a great diving catch from his centerfield position. Thanks, Luke, for the experience.

I used to love to watch Luke play. From T-ball through semi-pro it was one of the great joys of my life. Luke was actually a better ballplayer then I was. My "turtle-like" speed didn't help my game. With all due respect to Mickey, I enjoyed watching Luke more than I enjoyed watching Mickey.

I'm not sure I agree with the pressure "Mutt" put on Mickey in terms of a father's expectations. I guess with Mickey's ability and "Mutt's" coaching, a chance that is a million-to-one for most individuals came true.

"Mutt" passed away in 1952 after he had the chance to see his son play in Yankee Stadium alongside Joe DiMaggio and against both Ted Williams and Willie Mays. And as good as Luke was, my oldest daughter, Christine, was also pretty good. Christine distinguished herself by being the only player on her Little League team to play an entire season without striking out! Laura actually scored the only goal on her high school field hockey team.

Looking back to those days of my children's youth and mine, I still remember the outrageous behavior displayed by some parents, especially the fathers, who attended the Little League games. I've been around men in many situations—school, the military, construction, and corporations, but Little League fathers were "poster children" for bad behavior. They yelled at their children, belittled them, and created unrealistic expectations for them.

I had coached for several years and often was criticized by some parents because the kids on my team were "having too much fun." What were they supposed to have, if not fun? I hoped things would change, but sadly, if anything, they have gotten worse. Kids have enough pressure from a myriad of sources without having more added from a game that can bring unlimited joy. As Pink Floyd said, "Leave them Kids Alone!"

One last note on Mickey and Luke: After Luke finished college, he worked at Mickey Mantle's restaurant as a bartender/waiter for a while. Bill Lederman, the restaurant's owner, hired Luke immediately after I mentioned his baseball playing skills. Bill was a softball fanatic who pitched for the Mickey Mantle restaurant team that played in the Central Park League in New York City, so he thought that Luke might be a good addition to the team. Television host and political commentator Jerry Springer was a regular customer of Luke's at the bar. One day, as the *500 Home Run Club* was playing on the TV, Springer revealed that the video was one of his favorites. Talk about serendipity coming full circle and six degrees of separation. Mickey Mantle, Jerry Springer and Luke together. Great stuff. Couldn't make it up.

CHAPTER 16

FLESH, BLOOD, AND GRANITE

Perhaps my favorite Mickey Mantle photo appears in the book *Dynasty*, written in the 1970s by controversial Mantle author Peter Golenbock, whose 2007 book *Number 7: Mickey Mantle the Novel* was excoriated due to the fictionalized accounts of Mickey's sexual exploits, most notably with Marilyn Monroe. The Monroe story is doubtful since neither Mickey nor any of his sons ever mentioned it to me among the many negative comments they made about Joe DiMaggio. Seducing Joe D's wife would have been a tasty zinger toward the Yankee Clipper. In any event, the photo in *Dynasty*, which is an account of the 1949 - 1964 Yankees, the teams that steam rolled to 13 pennants and nine World Championships, showed Mickey catching a long fly ball in front of the three tombstone-like monuments in dead center field. The caption of the photo read, "4 Monuments, 3 in granite, 1 in flesh!"

I first saw the monuments while exiting Yankee Stadium. In the 1950s, fans could leave via exits in dead centerfield. I remember looking back as I reached the monuments and being stunned at the distance back to home plate (461 feet). The three monuments that I gazed up at were erected for, in order, legendary New York Yankees' manager Miller Huggins in 1932, Lou Gehrig in 1941 upon his tragic demise, and last the Sultan of Swat, Babe Ruth in 1949. Incidentally, Ruth once held Huggins by his ankles from a moving train. Good thing Miller was slight and Ruth strong; otherwise the monument might have been erected earlier.

The Yankees and Boston Red Sox have had a long and colored history, which has, at times, produced fascinating situations. When Mickey played center field for the Yankees, the Red Sox had one of the great defensive center fielders of all time, a player who is hardly mentioned anymore but who

140

was as good as Willie and better than Mickey defensively. That player, who Ted Williams said was the greatest outfielder he ever saw, was Jimmy Piersall.

Jimmy joined the Red Sox for a "cup of coffee" in 1950, appearing in six games. After doing well in the minors, he joined the Sox in 1952 as a part-time shortstop and right fielder. Jimmy was extremely high strung, partially because of the pressure his father put on him to be a major leaguer. Jimmy's mother had suffered from emotional problems, which continually forced her in and out a sanitarium. In 1952, Piersall took a bow after making a catch. It got worse.

Before a game against the Yankees on May 24 at Fenway Park, Piersall and Billy Martin exchanged barbs as Jimmy was playing shortstop during batting practice and Billy was loosening up on the sidelines. Billy invited Jimmy to settle things under the stands, which was an invitation that Jimmy readily accepted. The two fought, with Billy ripping Jimmy's shirt before Yankees' coach Bill Dickey and Sox hurler Ellis Kinder broke up the fight. But Jimmy wasn't finished.

When Piersall went to the Boston clubhouse, he had a brief altercation with teammate Mickey McDermott. A few days later, he disciplined Vern Stephens' four-year-old son by allegedly spanking him. Jimmy was sent to the minors and was soon institutionalized. Jimmy recovered, making a comeback in 1953 as the regular center fielder.

The monuments at the Stadium fascinated Jimmy. He had a specific goal with respect to his playing career, which was to catch a ball behind the monuments, hit by Mickey Mantle. "Why Mantle?" he was asked. "Well, who else is going to hit the SOB that far?"

Jimmy never caught a Mickey Mantle fly ball behind the monuments, but I remember Mickey going behind them in pursuit of a ball that Harry Simpson hit over his head. Another time, Bill Tuttle of the Tigers, not Jimmy Piersall, caught up to a Mickey drive near the monuments. Piersall never achieved his goal, although years later, when he was with Cleveland, Jimmy sat down behind the monuments with Mickey hitting, hoping to tempt the gods into helping Mickey hit the ball to him.

I recall Mickey standing at rapt attention in front of the monuments. It was a beautiful fall October day in 1957. It was my first World Series game so naturally I got to the stadium around 11:00 AM for the 2 o'clock start against the Milwaukee Braves. There was a band positioned in front of the monuments, which suddenly broke into the song "Oklahoma," from the hit 1940s play of the same name. Mickey was shagging balls in the outfield and when the song began, he suddenly took off his ball cap and stood at attention, facing the band and monuments. At the song's conclusion, he jogged out to the bandleader, shook his hand, and waved to the other musicians.

One night I told Mickey how my backyard in Yonkers was converted to miniature Yankee Stadium. I had even put three metal chairs in the far end of my yard, past the apple tree, to replicate the monuments. My backyard was the scene of marathon wiffle ball games. When batting, each kid would imitate the batting stance of the Yankee or opponent lineup. The longest ball hit landed on top of a tree in "right field" in my yard. Naturally, I hit it during my Mantle stance batting lefty. Reflecting, I'm sure I swung from the heels, like Mickey, opposed to slapping at the ball like Tony Kubek or Bobby Richardson.

Individuals who are icons often cannot understand why they are idolized. Mickey listened to my story and said that now, at the age of 60- something; he finally understood what we had done as kids when we pretended to be Mickey Mantle or Willie Mays or Stan Musial. Mutt, his father, had canonized Mickey Cochrane and as a youngster, Mickey said that he had hero-worshipped Stan Musial, ironically that when he became the icon, he wondered why fans thought he was worthy of adulation.

Wiffle ball brings back memories of Nicky DeVito, a "Goodfellas" type character from Yonkers, who will go down forever in the memory of my childhood friends for stabbing his idol, Yogi Berra. Nicky, while attempting to get Yogi's autograph after a game, thrust a sharp pencil in Yogi's direction that met Lawrence Peter Berra's palm. Thankfully, the injury wasn't serious, due to Yogi's sandpaper like callused hands. Nicky DeVito was also removed from 8th grade art class for continuing to refer to 19th century French painter George Seurat as "Sewer Rat." In 8th grade shop class he would eat his classmates' lunches or, if he didn't like the sandwich, he would put it in a vise and crush it. He finally was removed from that class for imitating the hand of our shop teacher, Benjamin Brooks, who had lost three fingers one year demonstrating how to use a power saw! Thanks for the memories Nicky DeVito; you should have a monument somewhere in Yonkers.

Mickey Mantle was turned into a granite monument on August 25, 1996. The game was a sellout before Yankee Stadium sellouts became commonplace. The crowd cheered for Mickey's surviving family - wife Merlyn, sons David and Danny, and their wives. I recently watched a tape of the event which gave me the feeling the huge ovations for the Mantle family was the fans' attempt to somehow reconnect with Mickey and show their affection. During the last few years, the media have referred to Mickey as The Most Beloved Yankee.

Yankee teammate, close friend and fellow Hall of Famer Whitey Ford unveiled the granite monument. Carved on the stone were the words: "A Great Teammate. A magnificent Yankee who left a legacy of unequalled courage."

Former New York Yankees' Manager Joe Torre was standing next to Whitey. He recalled that he had one of the greatest thrills of his career in his first major league spring training game. Looking up from his catcher's position, he saw a Number 7 on the broad back of a Yankees' player taking practice swings.

In a recent interview on cable's Major League Baseball Network, Torre, who was a Brooklyn Dodgers' fan, recalled Mantle's great catch of a Gil Hodges drive in the 1956 World Series that preserved Don Larsen's bid for a perfect game. Torre, who was sitting in the left field stands, said that Mantle and the ball were coming right toward him.

Actor-comedian Billy Crystal was also part of the ceremony. He related that his first Yankees game was May 30, 1956; the day Mickey hit the "green copper roof" the first time. Crystal also told of buying a seat from the old Yankee Stadium and having Mickey sign it years later. Mickey wrote, "I wish I was still playing, and you were still sitting here."

The Yankees won the regularly scheduled game that day. Special Rawlings baseballs, inscribed with the number 7, were used during the game, which was the first time in major league history that a ball had been inscribed with a player's number. The second time was when Cal Ripken broke Lou Gehrig's consecutive game streak.

For some reason, my memories of the real Yankee Stadium revolve around those monuments and the façade, which Mickey immortalized. The revamped Yankee Stadium (1973) has provided a very personal memory of Mickey appearing on the giant TV screen on Old Timer's Day 1995. Addressing the fans, as I had suggested to him during a call he had made to me while in a Dallas hospital that summer, Mickey said:

"Hi, this is Mick. When I left Baylor University Medical Center about six weeks ago, I felt great. I started working out on the treadmills, bicycles, etc. and I was doing great. I came back to the hospital for check-ups. About two weeks ago, the doctors found a couple of spots of cancer in my lungs. Now I'm taking chemotherapy to get rid of the new cancer. I'm hoping to get back to as good as I was right after the transplant. I'd like to again thank everyone for all the thoughts and prayers. And if you'd like to do something really great – be a donor."

As I watched the video screen, I saw not Mickey Mantle the baseball icon, but a person I cared for and wanted only the best for. It was not meant to be since Mickey passed away the next month. But seeing him, high above the monuments, speaking to the crowd was very special to so many people.

CHAPTER 17

MEMORIES IN MANTLE COUNTRY: MICKEY WAS BETTER THAN WE KNEW

I have many memories of seeing Mickey play, but seared in my consciousness, scattered among the great moments, is one painful early experience that demonstrated that even our best plans can be ruined. Uncle Chubby, "Mac," and I were driving along the Major Deegan Expressway on a bright, beautiful Sunday morning on our way to the Home of Champions with my ticket clutched in my hand.

We had left Yonkers at about 11 A.M. for the game, which had a 2:05 starting time. Since the ride is only 30 minutes under reasonable traffic conditions, we were going to wander around the souvenir shops on River Avenue before watching batting practice. It was a great plan with poor execution.

As we passed the Stella D'Oro factory on 238th Street, the aroma of fresh baking cookies and breads entered the car. It whet our appetites, not only for baked goods but for baseball. Then what often occurs on the Major Deegan, the Cross Bronx Expressway, the Long Island Expressway and most New York highways happened. Traffic ground to a halt.

We weren't too worried because we had a lot of time, or so we thought. Traffic crawled along as slowly as an old Washington Senators' season while time seemed to race by—11:45 AM, …12:20 PM, …1:05 PM. By now we were concerned and later learned that there had been an accident on the

George Washington Bridge. In 1958, there were no radio traffic reports every 10 minutes.

We crawled along slowly, changing lanes to the one that was moving a little better only to be frustrated as the lane we entered stopped moving as the one we left began to move. Okay, we can skip going to the souvenir shops. We would miss some batting practice. We still would make the game.

Finally, at about 1:50 PM, on our left, not too far away, we saw Yankee Stadium. On the right I gazed at the abandoned Polo Grounds as I hoped we could park the car and run into the Stadium, maybe even for the top of the first, but certainly for the bottom of the first when Mickey would be the third hitter. The traffic stopped again. It was excruciating.

I had that horrible feeling of complete helplessness, almost panic, as Mel Allen gave me, and a few hundred thousand-radio listeners the starting lineups. The Orioles were retired quickly without scoring in the top half of the first inning. Okay, I had missed the top of the first, but at least Baltimore didn't score, now the Yankees were coming to bat and ....

We got to the parking lot, paid our $2 (yes, that was the price), and started running towards Gate 4. I heard Bob Sheppard announce, "Batting third, number seven, Mickey Mantle, number seven." That was it. I was going to miss Mickey's first at bat. Thirty seconds later, as the ticket taker handed me back the stub, the crowd let out a tremendous roar, a roar reserved for Ruth, Gehrig, DiMaggio and Mantle.

I questioned the existence of God and remembered the old joke about how the man who saw his mother-in-law drive his new Cadillac off a cliff had felt. I felt terrible that I didn't see Mickey's home run although I felt great that Mickey had hit a home run.

I missed this one but I had seen many other Mickey Mantle home runs. I was lucky to have been at some of the games that were pivotal in his career or among his top thrills. Yankee Stadium is called "The House That Ruth Built," but Gehrig, DiMaggio, and then Mickey helped keep it in good repair. In the 1950s and 1960s, Mickey was in charge, a fact everyone knew.

On Mickey Mantle Day, a banner hanging from the upper third deck in right field simply stated, "This is Mantle Country." Batters rarely reached the upper deck in right field in the original Yankee Stadium, but Mickey was no ordinary batter and the third deck was no stranger to many of his home runs. I know that a home run that lands just beyond the outfielder's glove or one that travels 500 feet both count the same, but the impact, sound and especially the distance of a Mantle home run had a tremendous psychological effect on pitchers. Just ask Pete Ramos or Camilo Pascual. As Elvis used to sing, they were "all shook up".

Before I went into the military in 1966, I attended the annual Yankee Old Timers' Game. In the regularly scheduled game, Mickey, who was starting to slip as injuries and his lifestyle took their toll on his body, came up with the bases loaded against Detroit lefty Hank Aguirre. Batting right-handed, he hit a line drive into the upper third tier in right field. It was still rising as it crashed into the blue seats. Left-handed sluggers rarely reached these seats! Although Mickey could display it less often, his power had not diminished.

Mickey's opposite field power was mind-boggling. I had never seen or read about a right-handed batter reaching the right field upper deck in the original Yankee Stadium. Right-handed hitters like Harmon Killebrew, Frank Howard, Frank Robinson, Rocky Colavito, Roy Sievers, Gus Zernial, Jackie Jensen, Bob Cerv, Elston Howard, Bill "Moose" Skowron, Hank Bauer and even Gil McDougald hit home runs to right field, but not to the third deck the way Mickey did. Recently, inducted Hall-of-Famer Mike Piazza (2016) came closest to Mickey's opposite-field power.

Hall-of-Famer Brooks Robinson was asked if he ever experienced fear-playing baseball. "Yes, when Mickey Mantle is up batting right handed." Robinson went on to say that his extraordinary reflexes would have not protected him against a Mantle line drive heading straight at his head! It is well documented that the sound of a Mantle struck ball was a uniquely different sound than any other hitter. It was like an explosion.

I remember opening day in 1956. Mickey hit two home runs off Washington pitcher Camilio Pascual. Both traveled more than 450 feet to dead centerfield. President Eisenhower, who was at the game, visited with Mickey when it was over. Mickey gave "Ike" another thrill that year in the opener of the World Series when he homered his first at-bat against the Brooklyn Dodgers at Ebbets Field. Mickey was a favorite of the President. It had to please Mickey that he could provide thrills and excitement to another American hero.

Nineteen fifty-six created so many Yankees' memories for so many individuals that it ranks with the 1927, 1961 and 1998 seasons. The school year had just started when I arrived at my eighth grade class on the morning of September 19, 1956 wondering how the Yankees had done in Chicago the night before. I knew a win would have clinched the pennant. One of my buddies said, "They won in the 11th inning on Mickey's 50th." Mickey hit a home run off White Sox southpaw ace Billy Pierce to win the game, which eliminated the Sox, the last team that had a mathematical chance of overtaking the Yankees. It was the Yankees' 22nd pennant and Stengel's seventh in his eight years at the Yankees' helm. There were other statistics that will bring us to the present.

Mickey became only the second Yankee to hit 50 or more home runs in a season and only the 13th player to do it since 1901. Hitting at least 50 home runs in a season was a great feat. Lou Gehrig, Ted Williams, Joe DiMaggio, Stan Musial, Harmon Killebrew, Frank Howard, Frank Robinson and Duke Snider never did it.

The following table lists the players who have accomplished it and compares how their home run total compares to the average number of home runs hit by teams in the league.

Players With At Least 50 Home Runs in a Season from 1901-1956

YEAR	PLAYER	HRs	AVR HR/TEAM	% LEAGUE HRs
1927	Ruth	60	55	109%
1921	Ruth	59	60	99%
1932	Foxx	58	88	66%
1938	Greenberg	58	108	54%
1930	Wilson	56	112	50%
1920	Ruth	54	46	117%
1928	Ruth	54	50	109%
1949	Kiner	54	117	46%
1956	Mantle	52	134	39%
1947	Kiner	51	111	46%
1947	Mize	51	111	46%
1955	Mays	51	158	32%
1938	Foxx	50	108	46%

Examine Babe Ruth's 1927 season. When he set the single season home run record with 60 that year, the average American League team, *including* Ruth's Yankees, averaged 55 home runs. Ruth's 60 home runs, compared to the league average of 55 home runs, equaled 109 percent of the home runs hit by a 1927 American League team.

When Ruth hit 54 home runs in 1920, American League teams, including Ruth's Yankees, averaged 46 home runs. Ruth's 54 home runs were 17 percent *higher* than the American League *team* average of 46.

Mickey's 52 home runs in 1956 are in the lower part of the group since American League teams averaged 134 home runs that season, which meant that Mickey's 52 were 39 percent of the average team's home run total. When Willie Mays hit 51 in 1955, National League teams averaged 158 home runs, so Willie's total was only 32 percent of the National League team average.

In 1961, Roger hit 61 and Mickey hit 54. In 1965, Willie had 52. There were no more 50 home run seasons until George Foster exploded with 52 for Cincinnati in 1977. In 1990, Cecil Fielder hit 51 for the Tigers and that was it.

From 1901 through 1990, only 11 different players hit 50 or more home runs in a season. Those 11 players did it a total of 18 times. Then came 1994 and the strike, after which more rabbit was in the ball. Of course, we know that other reasons existed, as Jose Canseco, Mark McGwire and others have told us.

From 1995 through 2006, 13 different players hit 50 or more home runs 21 times. Let that sink in. In 93 seasons (1901-1993), 11 different players hit 50 or more home runs in a season 18 times. In the next 12 seasons (1995-2006), 13 different players hit 50 or more home runs in a season 21 times. Bud Selig and the baseball moguls must be told what Desi told Lucy. "Bud, you got a lot of 'splaining to do."

The following table lists the 50 or more home run seasons from 1995 until 2006. It compares a player's home run total to the home runs a team in the league averaged and graphically illustrates the inflation of the home runs hit by the modern player.

Players With At Least 50 Home Runs in a Season from 1995-2006

YEAR	PLAYER	HRs	AVR HR/TEAM	% LEAGUE HRs
2001	Bonds	73	185	40%
1998	McGwire	70	160	44%
1998	Sosa	66	160	41%
1999	McGwire	65	181	36%
2001	Sosa	64	185	35%
1999	Sosa	63	181	35%
2006	Howard	58	178	33%
1997	McGwire	58	155*	37%
2001	Gonzalez	57	185	31%
2002	Rodriguez	57	176	32%
1997	Griffey Jr.	56	177	32%
1998	Griffey Jr.	56	179	31%
2006	Ortiz	54	182	30%
1996	McGwire	52	196	27%
2001	Rodriguez	51	179	28%
2002	Thome	51	162	31%
2005	Jones	51	161	32%
1996	Anderson	50	196	26%
1995	Belle	50	155	32%
2000	Sosa	50	188	27%
1998	Vaughn	50	160	31%
			*ML Avg.	

The statistics are those of "arena" baseball, where there is little balance between offense and defense. When Babe Ruth hit 60 home runs to set the record, he hit 109 percent of the home runs (60 for Ruth, 55 was the team average) than teams in the league. When Barry Bonds hit 73 home runs, he hit 40 percent of the home runs (73 for Barry, 185 was the team average) National League teams averaged that season. Sammy Sosa hit more than 60 home runs in three different seasons and never even led the league. David Ortiz hit 54 home runs in 2006, which equals the most Mickey ever hit in a season, yet Ortiz, a designated hitter, was brushed aside when it came time to determine the league's MVP. A major reason David was brushed aside is because home runs have become so common.

The Yankees set the team home run record in 1961 with 240, a record that stood until—right, you guessed it—after the 1994 strike. In 1996, Oakland hit 243 home runs. That didn't set a record because Seattle hit 245 home runs that season. That didn't set a record because Baltimore hit 257 home runs for the new record.

Texas, a team that hit 221 home runs, had to be satisfied in tying the other league's record set in 1947 by New York (the Giants, not the Mets). The National League, without a designated hitter, saw Colorado hit 221 home runs to tie the 1947 Giants. Four American League teams and one National League team hit more than 200 home runs in 1996. Hey Bud, you got even more 'splaining to do.

Baltimore's single season home run lasted one season. In 1997, Seattle set a new record of 264 home runs and in 2000, Houston set the National League record by hitting 249 home runs. Teams hitting more than 200 home runs in a season are no longer unique.

Modern statistical analyses reveal just how great Mickey Mantle was when he was at his best. Michael Lewis in *Moneyball* defines sabermetrics as the specialized analysis of baseball through objective, empirical evidence. According to Bill James, sabermetrics is the search for objective knowledge about baseball. When the "experts" compared Mickey Mantle to Willie Mays, the first thing they mentioned was each player's batting average. Then they compared the number of home runs each player hit and that was usually followed by comparing their slugging averages. Finally, RBI totals and runs scored were cited.

Mantle struck out much more than Mays, which was considered a tremendous negative. Mantle walked much more than Mays, but on base average didn't become an official statistic until 1984. After each had retired, Mays was considered the greater offensive player, although it was generally conceded that when he was healthy, as he was for most of 1956, Mantle more than held his own against Mays.

In 2016, a player's offensive abilities are measured differently from the days of Mantle and Mays. Many of the recently created modern statistics fail to account for many variables and some might even be based on faulty premises, but they have made Mantle into a better offensive player than Mays, so more power to them.

Batting average is much less important today than it was when Mantle and Mays were active. Mantle finished at .298. Mays finished at .302. However, American Leaguers batted .256 during Mantle's career while National Leaguers hit .264 during Mays' career. Mantle hit 42 points higher than the league average. Mays batted 38 points above the league average. Of course, during the 1950s, the National League had many more great black players than the American League. Statistics are great.

Mantle's career on base average was .421 compared to Mays' .384. Each had a .557 slugging average. Mantle's best single-season slugging averages were .705 in 1956, .687 in 1961 and .665 in 1957. Mays' best were .667 in 1954, .659 in 1955 and .645 in 1965. The most home runs Mantle hit in a season was 54 in 1961. Mays' single-season high was 52 in 1965.

WAR, or Wins Above Replacement, purports to determine the number of wins a player added to the team above what a replacement player would add. A WAR value greater than eight is considered MVP quality and a value greater than five is All-Star quality. Mantle's top WAR values are 12.9, 12.5 and 11.9. Mays' best are 11.0, 10.6 and 10.4.

Mays played for 19 full seasons. In 1952 (army), 1972 and 1973, he was a part-time player. Mantle played 16 complete seasons. He missed much of 1963 when he broke his foot in a fence at Baltimore and played in only 96 games his rookie season. Mays' career WAR is 154.7. Mantle's is 120.2.

Offensive winning percentage purports to determine the percentage of games a team with nine of a specific player batting would win, assuming average pitching and defense. Mantle produced an .803 winning percentage compared to Mays' .748. Willie Mays was the most exciting player in the game when he wasn't batting. Mantle was the most exciting batter since the days of Babe Ruth and Lou Gehrig.

In 1958, I attended a World Series Game and observed perhaps the hardest ball I had ever seen Mickey hit. Batting right-handed, he hammered a Warren Spahn pitch off the scoreboard in left field. What made it remarkable was that the third baseman, Eddie Matthews, jumped for the line drive, which never got more than 10 feet off the ground as it crashed against the scoreboard 430 feet away. I still remember the loud thud that reverberated above the cheers of 65,000 people.

On Monday, August 15, 1960, I seated myself behind the on-deck circle on the visitor's side of the field to watch the Yankees play the Orioles. I was about to observe, up close, perhaps the pivotal game of Mickey's career. During most of the fifties, Mickey had been booed for a variety of reasons. He was going to be the next Joe DiMaggio, but with the exception of 1956, he hadn't lived up to his "DiMaggio like" expectations. Mickey was extremely hard on himself when he didn't meet the standards set for him. Yankee fans had a tough time relating to his on-field behavior, which was sometimes churlish. Many of them interpreted Mickey's actions as conceit, such as never tipping his cap or running with his head down. His modest Midwest demeanor was misunderstood. Casey Stengel didn't help matters by constantly criticizing Mickey to the press in terms of what "my center fielder could be!"

Writer David Halberstam, in *Memories of the Mick*, reflected, "More than any other athlete of his era, he was burdened by expectations, those of his father at first, then of his manager Casey Stengel, and finally his fans. No matter what he did, it was never good enough. No matter what he hit, he should have hit 30 points higher."

According to *The Yankee Encyclopedia, Volume 3*, Mickey's relationship with the fans changed at this game against the Birds. The previous day, the Yankees had lost a doubleheader to Washington to fall into third place, one-half game out of first. The doubleheader's nightcap was tied 3-3 in the top of the 15th inning when Ralph Terry hit Reno Bertoia on the wrist with a pitch. The Yankees disputed home plate umpire Charlie Berry's call, claiming the pitch had hit Reno's bat to no avail. Listening to the game at home, I hoped the pitch really had hit Reno's bat because then I would have been certain he hadn't been injured and the potential lead run wouldn't have been on base. Reno was fine. He went to first base, igniting a Senators' three run rally. The Yankees failed to score in bottom of the 15th inning, but something had happened in that second game that upset me much more than the Yankees' doubleheader loss.

In the sixth inning, with score 1-1, Clete Boyer led off with a single. Roger Maris followed with one of his own, to put Yankees runners at the corners with no outs. Hector Lopez hit a hard ground ball to shortstop Jose Valdivielso, who flipped the ball to second baseman Billy Gardner. Roger slid hard into second, breaking up the double play as Boyer scored the lead run, but Gardner's knee went into Roger's ribs, forcing him to leave the game.

Mickey was the batter with Lopez on first and one out. Batting right-handed against lefty Jack Kralick, Mickey hit a ground ball to third base that Reno Bertoia fielded. He fired to second to start an around the horn double play that shouldn't have been a double play. Mickey didn't run all the way to first base. Mickey Mantle did not run out the ground ball. Casey Stengel reacted immediately. He replaced Mickey with Bob Cerv. After the game, Stengel was still piqued. "I took him out because he didn't run and I'm tired of seeing him not run. If he can't run, he should tell me." The fact that Mickey had previously said that he was, "not hurting" didn't help matters.

I had to attend the Yankees' next game to see what would happen for myself. It started out badly. Mickey was booed vociferously when Bob

Sheppard announced his name. I sat there silently. One of the Orioles young phenoms, Jerry Walker, started against Yankees' right-hander Art Ditmar. Ron Hansen hit a solo home run in the second inning for a 1-0 Orioles lead. Then in the third, former Yankee Gene Woodling singled home Gene Stephens, who had singled and stolen second. In the fourth, the Yankees tied the game. *New York Times* baseball writer Louis Effrat succinctly described my emotions as well as those of most the fans when he wrote, "The Orioles lead lasted until the fourth and the way the Yankees tied it up must have thrilled those to whom Mantle is dear. Hector Lopez led off with an infield single and Mickey smashed the ball against the second wire fence in the right field Yankee bullpen for a 400-foot homer. As Mickey trotted across the plate and headed toward the dugout, he tipped his cap to the fans. That comes under the heading of a rarity."

Knuckle ball pitcher Hoyt Wilhelm replaced Walker on the mound as Orioles' catcher Clint Courtney switched to the oversized catcher's glove that manager Paul Richards had designed in an attempt to improve the catcher's chances of handling the knuckler. The score remained knotted at 2-2 until Jackie Brandt hit an eighth inning home run for a one run Orioles lead, which didn't last long. In the Yankees' eighth, Hector Lopez worked Wilhelm for a walk, bringing up Mickey, who immediately was down in the count, no balls and two strikes. Mickey swung at the next delivery, lifting a high, foul pop up in front of the grandstand behind home plate. I was so close to the action that I could see Courtney having trouble because of the large glove. The fans and I screamed as loud as we could, "Drop it, drop it." He did. Given a new life, Mickey fouled off the next pitch and then, on the next knuckle ball, a pitch that had always given Mickey problems, he hit a screaming line drive into the right field seats to put the Yankees ahead. The cheers made the reaction after Mickey's first home run seem reserved. I went crazy! What a night after the booing to start the game.

The Yankee Encyclopedia continues, "The New York press wrote the next day of all Mickey's attributes, including his courage in playing with painful injuries, and he was never booed again at Yankee Stadium." Roger Maris eventually won the MVP award, but Casey declared that Mantle deserved the honor, because of his grit, courage, ability and friendliness with teammates. Mickey was the most popular guy on the Yankees. By the end of his career, Mickey may have been the most popular player in Yankees' history.

That same year, 1960, I saw Mickey hit a memorable home run against the Pittsburgh Pirates in the World Series. Batting right-handed, he cleared the 436-foot sign in right centerfield. Pirates' center fielder Bill Virdon noted that, "Mantle's blow went at least 50 feet above the fence and was still going when I last saw it." In my memory, Mickey was at his peak in that World Series. Everything he hit was a screaming line drive. He batted .400 but couldn't prevent a seven game loss. They say he cried after the game seven … immortalized in the movie *A Bronx Tale*. "Mickey Mantle cried" were words that come out of the Robert DiNiro's 12-year-old son's disbelieving mouth. I was devastated. It is bad enough to lose, but this was a difficult loss to accept.

The 1960 World Series was a nightmare. The fact that Mickey cried after the Yankees lost reveals how deeply he felt about his team. Batting .400, slugging .800, hitting three home runs and using his baseball instincts to get the Yankees to the fateful Pittsburgh half of the ninth inning were meaningless, because the Yankees lost.

I still remember seeing Pirates' outfielder Gino Cimoli, a former Brooklyn Dodger, gloat in a television interview. "They set the records, but we won the game."

The Yankees set a World Series team record by batting .338 to the Pirates .256. The Yankees outscored the Bucs 55-27, hit 10 home runs to the Pirates four, scored in double figures in three games and had a 3.54 ERA compared to the Pirates 7.11. Bobby Richardson set a record with 12 RBIs to become the first player on a losing team to be selected Series MVP. The Pirates were the World Champions.

Mickey not only had great physical talent. He was a smart player. It was the top of the ninth inning of Game Seven with the Yankees trailing, 9 -7. Bob Friend, the Pirates ace whom the Yankees had belted around in his two starts but the pitcher most considered the Pirates best next to Vern Law, replaced Elroy Face on the mound. Richardson greeted Friend with a base hit. Dale Long, a powerful left handed hitting former Pirate pinch-hitting for Joe DeMaestri, singled to right to put the potential tying runs on base with Roger Maris the batter.

Lefty Harvey Haddix relieved Friend. He got Maris on a foul out, bringing up Mickey. Batting from the right side against the crafty southpaw, Mickey singled to right, scoring Richardson and moving Long, with the potential tying run, to third. It was on the next play that Mickey would show that he was more than a slugger.

Yogi was the batter. Everyone knew that he was a pull hitter. Sure enough, he hit a sharp ground ball down the first base line where first baseman Rocky Nelson was playing on the bag, holding Mickey on. Nelson grabbed Yogi's shot and instead of firing to second for the force out, he stepped on first base to retire Berra for the second out and *remove* the force on Mickey.

Nelson, recognizing his mental mistake, lunged to tag Mickey, who was a few feet off the base. Mantle realized that he couldn't make it to second as Gil McDougald, who had pinch-run for Long at third was racing home with the tying run. Mickey made a headlong dive into the base in order to avoid Nelson's tag. He succeeded.

Mickey knew instantly that when Nelson stepped on first to retire Yogi, the force play at second was removed. He had the right to return to first base because Berra was out. Instead of going for second, Mickey alertly returned to first, allowing the tying run to score. It was all for naught, but it gave the Yankees life.

There is an intriguing sidelight to the home run that ended that Series. Andy Jerpe, a 14-year-old schoolboy that was in a vacant lot outside Forbes Field, retrieved the ball Bill Mazeroski hit. Andy took the ball to the Pirates' dressing room to present it to Mazeroski. The second baseman autographed the ball. He then performed an act that is the antithesis of the 21st century.

"You keep it son. The memory is good enough for me."

I remember two dramatic pinch-hit home runs in the 60s. On May 23, 1962 Mickey hit a pinch-hit three run homer against the Indians in Cleveland after being injured for a long period of time. As Mickey limped around the bases, I jumped up and banged my head against my Uncle Chubby's chin, who was peering over my shoulder. I felt so bad. This was the uncle who had turned me on to baseball and the Yankees!

The other pinch-hit I remember was seen by many of my family members. All the men were around the TV, watching as the Yankees were losing to the Orioles in an early September game in 1963. Yankee second baseman Bobby Richardson describes the moment in the book *Sweet Seasons*:

"Mickey was out of the line-up for two months with a broken ankle. We came down to our final out and Ralph Houk told Mickey to 'grab a bat.' Mickey couldn't believe it, but he went to the bat rack and what followed was one of the most incredible scenes I've ever seen on a ball field.

"Some of the fans could see into the dugout, and when they saw Mickey grab a bat, they passed the word. Within a few seconds everyone in the park knew Mantle was hitting, and when he walked out of the dugout, he was greeted with the most thunderous applause I've ever heard. I was in the on-deck circle at the time. Mickey was very moved. He said to me 'I hope I can at least hit a single for them.'

"Then he stepped into the batter's box but couldn't hit because the crowd wouldn't stop cheering. He had to step out several times before they quieted down. Finally he got into the batter's box, and batting right-handed hit a game tying home run. That thunderous ovation rose again and didn't die down for ten minutes. Mickey was a true folk hero and the fans loved him."

Perhaps my greatest memory in Mantle country was during the third game of the 1964 World Series. I was seated high up in the third deck in right field. The façade was directly above me. Mickey, playing right field because of his now limited range, was below me. He had made an error earlier in the game, which was now in the bottom of the ninth, with the Yankees and St. Louis Cardinals tied 1-1.

The Cardinals brought in Barney Schultz, their ace knuckleballer relief pitcher as Mickey watched from the on-deck circle. It was later reported that he told Yankee catcher Elston Howard, "You might as well go on back to the clubhouse because I'm going to hit one out!"

What I recall 52 years later is Mickey's approach to home plate after Schultz finished his warm-up pitches. I had heard the Yankee Stadium fans cheer Mickey on so many occasions, but this cheer was like no other. It was as if by sheer will the 64,000 fans were demanding a home run. This was Yankee Stadium in October, with bright sunlight in the deep outfield, shadows draping over the infield and home plate in deep shade.

In an instant it was over. David Halberstam, in his book *1964*. described the scene:

"Behind the plate, Tim McCarver watched the ball float toward him, ever so slowly, ever so ominously. A number of things flashed through McCarver's mind in that instant, none of them good. He could see Barney Schultz very clearly, he could see the Cardinal's infielders, and he could almost feel the awesome physical surge in Mantle. For a split second, McCarver wanted to stop the scenario, to reach out and interfere with Mantle's bat, but then the ball floated in, and Mantle absolutely crushed it, a tape measure job well into the third tier in right field …."

And headed straight for Tom Molito.

I'd like to say I caught the ball, only it soared just over my right shoulder, crashing into a seat. Perhaps one day a Zapruder-like photo analysis will be able to zoom in and capture and verify my presence. The only witness was my younger cousin, whom I picked up from the back and almost choked to death as I bounced him up and down as we cheered.

The game-winning homer was Mickey's 16th in World Series play, which broke Babe Ruth's record. It was also the day that a large percentage of that crowd and Yankee fans everywhere nominated Mickey for canonization, or at least knighthood in Mantle Country.

CHAPTER 18

SORRY ABOUT MICKEY, DAD

The morning of August 13, 1995 broke clear and sunny. I had fallen asleep in our guestroom the previous night. When I got up, I groggily rolled over to turn the radio on. I heard the name "Mantle" and a cold chill surrounded me. I knew immediately that Mickey had died during the night. I had been hearing the dire medical reports all week, but as is often the case, the stark reality was still a shock. As someone said on television that day, "our childhood had officially ended." The word "our" referred to the millions of baby boomers that had grown up with Mickey and never outgrew him.

Luke wandered into the guestroom and simply said," Sorry about Mickey, dad." Kathleen, Christine and Laura gave me hugs. I'm sure the scene was repeated across America. During the day, President Clinton and former President Bush paid tribute to Mickey. Flags were hung at half-mast at Yankee Stadium, where legendary Yankee public address announcer Bob Sheppard simply said, "Today we have lost one of our own and one of the greatest baseball players in baseball history." His voice had never sounded so mournful. He would never again announce his favorite name the same way. Bob Sheppard announcing the 1950s and 1960s Yankee lineup still resonates in my mind, "Batting third… playing centerfield… number 7… Mickey Mantle… number 7." A member of the family in millions of American households was gone. Americans of all ages spent countless hours watching him and talking about him. He was bonding-glue that triggered moments of being together with a father, uncle, brother or friends.

All the newspapers the next day had Mickey on the front page. There were special sections within the paper. Naturally, they all became part of my collection. In the recent book, *Our Mickey*, by my friend Bill Lederman,

Mickey's restaurant partner, several quotes illustrated Mickey's appeal across all facets of society.

Tennis great John McEnroe: "My greatest sports hero of all time is Mickey Mantle. I just loved watching him. Every kid in my neighborhood in Douglaston (Queens, N.Y.) wanted to grow up to be Mickey Mantle."

Juan Marichal, Hall of Fame pitcher from the Dominican Republic: "In my country, we used to gather around a portable radio in the streets and listen to the game of the week. We would be talking and cheering for the players, mostly the Yankees except when Mickey came up. Then we would all get quiet. We just wanted to hear the sound of the baseball hitting the bat when Mickey was up."

Donald Trump, entrepreneur, made possibly my favorite quote from someone who is always seeking the spotlight: "I got to meet Mickey on one of those Yankee Old Timers Games. I had seen him play when I was a kid, but this was just as exciting for me to be sitting next to him. You could see he was really something special by the way everyone gathered around him. There was never *a star bigger than Mickey.*"

Mickey's monument at Yankee Stadium has the following: "A Great Teammate." He was just that. He was the Yankees' leader, on and off the field, in many ways even before Ralph Houk anointed him in 1961. It is well documented how Mantle went out of his way to make Elston Howard, the Yankee's first black player, accepted by his teammates. During spring training that year, 1954, Mickey ate lunch with Howard on the Yankee bus, symbolically not entering the "whites only" restaurant. The rest of the team followed his lead and took their food out to join Mickey and Elston on the bus.

Mickey also laid a red carpet leading to Howard's locker after "Ellie's" first game winning hit. Throughout his career, Mantle was loved by his teammates, black, white and Hispanic. Mickey's heart was in the right place when it came to race relations, but in his later years his drinking and warped sense of humor did not serve him well.

I had spoken with Mickey while he was hospitalized in Dallas in June. I had heard the hospital had been overwhelmed with over 25,000 get-well cards and miscellaneous items for their famous patient.

On June 8, 1995, Mickey received a transplant to replace a liver ravaged by cirrhosis, hepatitis C and the cancer that would soon cost him his life. Mickey finally, thankfully, finally realized what he meant to all of us.

Tom Molito

In early August 1995, doctors at Baylor University Medical Center in Dallas discovered that cancer had spread to other parts of his body. The drugs that he had been taking to prevent rejection of the transplanted liver had weakened Mickey's immune system, making it easier for the cancer to spread. The public reacted:

You need to get better -- fast. Not for you so much, but for thousands like me who can live with assassinations, Vietnam, and bombings, but can't stand the thought of losing THE MICK. Please get better quickly. Hell, I'd give you my own liver - you gave us your heart! You were, and ARE, the greatest, my friend.
Richard G. Good Sr.

As a boy growing up in the "fifties," you were my hero. My feelings toward Mickey Mantle were more than idolizing a baseball player. You made my life more exciting, more pleasant, more rewarding, and a thousand other adjectives too numerous to mention. These feelings have not dimmed over the years.
Bruce Lippy

There's one thing cancer *can't* take from you -- your millions of fans.
Jim Tewey
And Mickey reacted:
Mickey C. Mantle
Dallas, Texas
August 9, 1995
Dear Friends and Fans:

During my eighteen years as a New York Yankee I felt blessed that I could play baseball, a game I love so much. God gave me the strength, talent, and courage to play the game the way I felt it should be played. But it was my teammates that gave me the support and friendship I needed to find my place among great players, coaches, and managers. Until I entered the Betty Ford Clinic in January of 1994 to overcome my problem with alcohol, and, then underwent my liver transplant in June of 1995 at Baylor University Medical Center, I did not think that I would ever experience that kind of support and friendship again. I was wrong.

I entered the Betty Ford Clinic embarrassed and regretful that I had let

161

alcohol abuse effect (sic) my life, my family and my career. Those regrets continue, but because of you, your letters, cards, and prayers I once again felt an overwhelming rush of support and friendship. Again, I was overwhelmed.

With this letter to you many friends and fans that gave me the support and friendship I needed, I want to say that it meant the world to me. You were my teammates in my most difficult times. You picked me up and helped me to continue. You kept me in the game when I had my doubts. For that, and all the support I enjoyed during my years as an active player, I say, "Thank You" from the bottom of my heart. Thanks for being there....

Your Teammate
Mickey

One of the newspaper accounts had mentioned the name of his doctor who headed up the medical team. I figured Mickey had a lot of down time in bed and perhaps some *Cabin Fever Entertainment* videos would help pass the time. My secretary, Denise Bucci Iobbi, helped me select a variety of tapes we knew Mickey would like, such as Country Music, fishing and western films. We also included a bunch of movies for the doctors and nurses who were caring for Mickey. We were concerned our box wouldn't get through the avalanche of mail so we came up with an idea. Why not send the box to his doctor!"

Several days later, Denise buzzed me that Mickey was on hold. The call was to thank us for the tapes that the hospital staff was enjoying. The annual Old Timer's Game was coming up the following month, so I asked Mickey if he were going to be able to attend. Mickey said his doctors would not allow him to travel. He'd have to miss his first Old Timer's Game since he retired in 1969. I told him the fans would really miss him, but I had a thought. "Why don't you videotape a message that the Yankees could play on their jumbo TV in centerfield." "Hey, Tom, good idea. But do me a favor; don't tell anyone with the Yankees that it was your idea! They think I'm as dumb as a stump and I would never come up with a good idea." He laughed.

Pure Mickey, honest, self-deprecating and funny! He asked me what I thought he should say. I gave him a few thoughts, told him the welcome sign was still out in Bedford, and that I'd see him when he came to New York. It was not to be. I would never speak to Mickey again.

On Old Timer's Day, Mickey's video message was played to the 50,000 plus spectators. He thanked the fans for their support and encouragement during his illness. He also did a short presentation for organ donation, emphasizing the importance of donations. The crowd gave Mickey what was to be his final ovation at the conclusion of the speech.

That night I reflected on what had happened during the afternoon. I had actually helped Mickey say goodbye to America and his fans, which gave me great satisfaction, but it I would have preferred that it hadn't been necessary. If someone had told me in the 1950s that I somehow would be involved in Mickey Mantle's last appearance at Yankee Stadium, I would have dismissed the notion as pure daydreaming. I had come full circle from the hero-worshipping little boy to an adult who actually had Mickey Mantle in his life.

After death, Mickey actually became more popular than when he was living. Like Elvis, Marilyn Monroe, JFK and James Dean, he entered the world of mythology and folk legend. Politicians, movie stars, business leaders and other celebrities had sought out Mickey from all walks of life. Once, out of the clear blue, I asked Mickey if he had ever met Elvis Presley. I was curious if the two had met. Elvis was a great influence on my life because of his music, and I always linked Mickey with Elvis, since both shared the spotlight in 1956. Mickey said he never met Elvis and wondered why I asked. I told him that, "you both had to deal with iconic fame that the normal person could never understand".

I thought Mickey Mantle and Jerry Garcia of the Grateful Dead had very little in common, except that they died in close chronological time span. Robert Sullivan, a neighbor of mine in Bedford and editor for *Life Magazine*, wrote the following tribute:

Requiem of a Hero…
"He was born to his talent and his trade. He was an American traditionalist. He was an unassuming prodigy. He gained early fame and revolutionized his game; he was Huck Finn, charismatic - but also, he was made for our age and drew millions of kids to the area; he was beloved by his teammates and only reluctantly assumed the role of leader; uneasy in the spotlight, he was head down modest after stunning his audience with an awesome solo shot; by nature he was a happy man - but a man with pain and conflict; his weaknesses were apparent - he abused his body regularly, contributing his too early death; he died gracefully, trying to get well; he was mourned by his generation, and by those both older and younger, he was a giant, an original, an American beauty. He was not just admired by his fans

he was loved. He was Mickey Charles Mantle, the Mick and Captain Trips,"
Jerome Jerry Garcia.

Mickey's funeral was on national television from Dallas. Reflecting on Mickey's funeral, I wish they had had it in New York City. It would have given Mickey's legion of fans one last opportunity to say their last goodbye. It's only my own speculation, but I think the crowd size would have been historic. Perhaps Merlyn Mantle, who shared Mickey with America their entire lives, wanted just to bring him home to Dallas.

His old buddy, Bob Costas, gave the eulogy that perfectly captured what millions of baby boomers were feeling:

"I'm here today not so much to speak for myself as to simply represent the millions of baseball loving kids who grew up in the 50s and 60s and for whom Mickey Mantle was baseball. And more than that, he was a presence in our lives, a fragile hero to whom we had an emotional attachment so strong and lasting that it defied logic. Mickey often said he didn't understand it, this enduring connection and affection, the men in their forty's and fifty's otherwise perfectly sensible who went dry in the mouth and stammered like schoolboys in the presence of Mickey Mantle. And in the end people got it. And Mickey Mantle got something other than misplaced and mindless celebrity worship. He got something far more meaningful. He got love. Love for what he had been, love for what he had made us feel, love for the humanity and sweetness that was always there mixed in the flaws and all the pain that racked his body and his soul."

Thanks Bob Costas. Back in 1988, somebody commented that Costas and I looked like bug eyed little boys, staring at Mickey while *Cabin Fever Entertainment* was filming the *500 Home Run Club* video. It was true. Mickey's courage urging people not to be like him gave his fans one more heroic moment, perhaps his finest.

CHAPTER 19

"WHAT HE COULD HAVE BEEN"

It's hard to believe that over two decades have gone by since Mickey's death. As the years pass, it only increases my appreciation of my experiences with him. I continue to meet people, usually men my age, and occasionally females, who will always have a special place in their minds and hearts for Mickey Mantle.

I started this memoir in the late summer of 2013. Recently, we had some family friends over for lunch. My ears perked up when I heard a woman in the next room proclaim that, "Mickey Mantle had recently died." I naturally wandered into the room and corrected her chronological error. "I'm talking about Mickey Mantle, my dog," she laughingly explained. She continued that she had named the dog as a tribute to her, "All-time favorite guy."

It continues to astonish me how often I meet someone who had the same feelings as I do about Mickey. These individuals cut across all walks of life. Somehow we start talking sports, then baseball, and one of us mentions Mickey Mantle. At that point, the bond develops and we share our memories.

The one common thread that runs through a lot of these conversations was Mickey's bad knees and various injuries during his playing days. The phrase, "He could have been the greatest player of all time" usually is acknowledged. According to a recent book, *The All-Century Team*, released by Major League Baseball, "No one makes the All-Century Team based on what he could have been."

No, Mickey Mantle didn't make the All-Century Team based on what he could have been. He made it on what he had been, but one more "what-if".

Despite the "what-ifs," Mickey's statistics speak for themselves. His greatest disappointment though was not batting .300 lifetime. Sometime in July 1968 he had fallen below that numerical standard of excellence. I once calculated that Mickey needed 16 more lifetime hits to have a .300 batting average. That comes out to 1.1 hits a year over his 18 seasons. I made the mistake of telling Mickey my calculations and he responded, "Why the hell did you tell me that. Now I feel really bad." He was right. I should have kept the statistic to myself.

Entering the 1968 season, Mickey had 7,667 official plate appearances with 2.312 hits for a .302 lifetime batting average. Now Mark Twain, not a baseball fan but a pretty smart fellow, quoted Benjamin Disraeli when discussing statistics. "There are three kinds of lies: lies, damn lies, and statistics." The fact remains that Mickey hit .298, not .300. While one never knows when one hit can win a World Championship, Mickey's home runs, clutch hits, base running and defense were much more important that the .002 difference between batting .300 and .298.

Mickey's legs were his Achilles heel (his ankles also were a problem after he broke a bone in his foot when he ran into and got stuck in a chain link fence in Baltimore in June 1963). When Mickey hit a single to the outfield that might have been stretched into a double, he was wise enough not to risk potential problems and settled for the one base. If Mickey had only five more doubles a season, his slugging average would have increased to .568, which have placed him 15th on the all-time list, just behind Alex Rodriguez.

On several occasions I had mentioned the "Death Valley" dimensions of the original Yankee Stadium (pre-1974). I even reminded Mickey of several balls he hit in both the 1960 and 1963 World Series that traveled well over 425 feet but were just loud outs. The original Stadium had white markings on the black walls of 457 to left center, 461 to straight away center and 433 to right center. Harmon Killebrew, the great Minnesota Twins' slugger, told Mickey and Mickey repeated it on the *500 Home Run Club* video, "How the hell do you play here!"

I never heard Mickey complain about his home ballpark's dimensions. It wasn't his style to make excuses. In an audiotape, *Instant Replay: The Life and Legend of Mickey Mantle*, part of the Miley Collection, Mickey humbly stated that he and Whitey Ford estimated that he hit a minimum of 10 balls a year that became long outs in the cavernous Yankee Stadium outfield. They would have been home runs in any other park. Over 18 seasons, we are talking about possibly 180 home runs and close to 180 more hits. Mickey might have had well over 700 home runs and batted .307.

In 2000, *Yankees Magazine* had an article that addressed what Mickey could have been. "From September 28, 1968, the last day of his final at bat, until now, the closing notes of Mantle's career have sustained a symphony in its last measure but lacking a grace note. Because of what the Mick did, and perhaps more important, of what he did not do. Mantle remains real and will continue to be long after his fellow Hall of Famers are only ghostly impressions on their plaques in Cooperstown." "In this, Mantle is very different from most departed players. As the years of their activity become more distance and the memory of their play becomes less and less distinct, ballplayers as people are essentially forgotten, their existence reduced to a skeleton of statistics."

Mickey Mantle is largely immune from this phenomenon. In his case, there is an understanding that we can look at the numbers but they will be unequal to telling his story. Thanks to television, many more fans saw Mickey Mantle play than ever saw Babe Ruth, Ty Cobb or Joe DiMaggio. The generation raised on the memories of those viewers and the awe that they retain from the first day they first saw him in fuzzy black and white sends a very clear message to those who did not see him play. To those who did not get to appreciate his athleticism first hand, statistics cannot possibly convey how good he was.

In fact, the Mantle who was idolized and romanticized in the 50s and the 60s is as lost to later generations as the city of Atlantis. Despite his many accomplishments, the oral tradition of Mickey Mantle is one of "almost" and "could have been."

In the end, Mantle's "what-ifs," make him the rare baseball player of whom it can be said that there are hidden depths to his story. Mantle can't be reduced to statistics, he will always bear greater investigation, which means that he has transcended death and become what he should have been, a figure of myth, a legend. "Mickey Mantle lives within us still."

EPILOGUE

It has been more than 20 years since Mickey Mantle passed away. With the passage of time, perspective develops. I was extremely fortunate to have known Mickey Mantle, both the athlete and the person. I quickly discovered that Mickey was a good guy who loved people. He also loved a good time, was a great competitor, and was a person who was always completely honest, which was a trait that he required of his friends. Mickey loved to make fun at his own expense as much as he loved to "put on" people. He was obsessed with his mortality, which explains the times he acted in a manner that embarrassed him. Kathleen told me that she considered Mickey to be paradoxical -- he was simple, down to earth, and uncomplicated in a positive way, and yet he was worldly and sophisticated.

At his final press conference at Baylor University, the real Mickey Mantle was exposed to the world. Americans often put an individual on a pedestal in order to knock him off it. At his press conference, Mickey tried to help the American public knock him off his pedestal by telling everyone that all his did his entire life was "take, take, take," and now he wanted to "give." Mickey, with great courage, facing the dark part of the reality that was Mickey Mantle, pointed to himself and simply said, "This is a role model: Don't be like me."

When I think about Mickey Mantle, it is as if there were two Mickey Mantles. There was the Mickey Mantle that everyone saw as Number 7, and then there was the person from Oklahoma, who lived in Manhattan and with whom I spent time. When Mickey and I socialized, I would sometimes forget who he was. For me, that wasn't easy, but Mickey put people at ease, even friends who were his most ardent fans.

I wrote this book with the hope that Mickey Mantle fans could vicariously experience what it was like to double date with Mickey. I sincerely hope that a part of Mickey Mantle's life that I shared in provides greater insight into a baseball player who has become an American icon.

Tom Molito
June 2015

APPENDIX

MICKEY MANTLE'S BATTING RECORD

YEAR	G	AB	RUNS	HITS	2B	3B	HR	RBI	BB	SO	BA	OBA	SLG
1951	96	341	61	91	11	5	13	65	43	74	0.267	0.349	0.443
1952	142	549	94	171	37	7	23	87	75	111	0.311	0.394	0.530
1953	127	461	105	136	24	3	21	92	79	90	0.295	0.398	0.497
1954	146	543	129	163	17	12	27	102	102	107	0.300	0.408	0.525
1955	147	517	121	158	25	11	37	99	113	97	0.306	0.431	0.611
1956	150	533	132	188	22	5	52	130	112	99	0.353	0.464	0.705
1957	144	474	121	173	28	6	34	94	146	75	0.365	0.512	0.665
1958	150	519	127	158	21	1	42	97	129	120	0.304	0.443	0.592
1959	144	541	104	154	23	4	31	75	93	126	0.285	0.390	0.514
1960	153	527	119	145	17	6	40	94	111	125	0.275	0.399	0.558
1961	153	514	132	163	16	6	54	128	126	112	0.317	0.448	0.687
1962	123	377	96	121	15	1	30	89	122	78	0.321	0.486	0.605
1963	65	172	40	54	8	0	15	35	40	32	0.314	0.441	0.622
1964	143	465	92	141	25	2	35	111	99	102	0.303	0.423	0.591
1965	122	361	44	92	12	1	19	46	73	76	0.255	0.379	0.452
1966	108	333	40	96	12	1	23	56	57	76	0.288	0.389	0.538
1967	144	440	63	108	17	0	22	55	107	113	0.245	0.391	0.434
1968	144	435	57	103	14	1	18	54	106	97	0.237	0.385	0.398
		AB	RUNS	HITS	2B	3B	HR	RBI	BB	SO	BA	OBA	SLG
Career	2401	8102	1677	2415	344	72	536	1509	1733	1710	0.298	0.421	0.557

MICKEY MANTLE'S FIELDING RECORD

YEAR	POS	G	TC	TC/G	PO	A	E	DP	FLD%
1951	OF	86	145	1.7	135	4	6	1	0.959
1952	3B	1	4	4.0	1	1	2	0	0.500
1952	OF	141	374	2.7	347	15	12	5	0.968
1953	OF	121	338	2.8	322	10	6	2	0.982
1953	SS	1	0	0.0	0	0	0	0	0.000
1954	2B	1	2	2.0	2	0	0	0	1.000
1954	OF	144	356	2.5	327	20	9	5	0.975
1954	SS	4	10	2.5	5	5	0	1	1.000
1955	CF	145	385	2.7	372	11	2	2	0.995
1955	SS	2	4	2.0	4	0	0	0	1.000
1956	CF	144	384	2.7	370	10	4	3	0.990
1957	CF	139	337	2.4	324	6	7	1	0.979
1958	CF	150	344	2.3	331	5	8	2	0.977
1959	CF	143	375	2.6	366	7	2	3	0.995
1960	CF	150	338	2.3	326	9	3	1	0.991
1961	CF	150	363	2.4	351	6	6	0	0.983
1962	OF	117	223	1.9	214	4	5	1	0.978
1963	CF	52	102	2.0	99	2	1	0	0.990
1964	OF	132	225	1.7	217	3	5	1	0.978
1965	LF	108	174	1.6	165	3	6	0	0.966
1966	OF	97	174	1.8	172	2	0	0	1.000
1957	1B	131	1188	9.1	1089	91	8	82	0.993
1958	1B	131	1286	9.8	1195	76	15	91	0.988

Career	POS	G	TC	TC/G	PO	A	E	DP	FLD%
CF Totals		1073	2628	2.4	2539	56	33	12	0.987
OF Totals		838	1835	2.2	1734	58	43	15	0.977
1B Totals		262	2474	9.4	2284	167	23	173	0.991
LF Totals		108	174	1.6	165	3	6	0	0.966
SS Totals		7	14	2	9	5	0	1	1.000
2B Totals		1	2	2	2	0	0	0	1.000
3B Totals		1	4	4	1	1	2	0	0.500
TOTALS		2290	7131	3.1	6734	290	107	201	0.985

MISCELLANEOUS MICKEY MANTLE STATISTICS

YEAR	SB	CS	SB%	AB/HR	AB/K	AB/RBI
1951	8	7	53%	26.2	4.6	5.2
1952	4	1	80%	23.9	4.9	6.3
1953	8	4	67%	22.0	5.1	5.0
1954	5	2	71%	20.1	5.1	5.3
1955	8	1	89%	14.0	5.3	5.2
1956	10	1	91%	10.3	5.4	4.1
1957	16	3	84%	13.9	6.3	5.0
1958	18	3	86%	12.4	4.3	5.4
1959	21	3	88%	17.5	4.3	7.2
1960	14	3	82%	13.2	4.2	5.6
1961	12	1	92%	9.5	4.6	4.0
1962	9	0	100%	12.6	4.8	4.2
1963	2	1	67%	11.5	5.4	4.9
1964	6	3	67%	13.3	4.6	4.2
1965	4	1	80%	19.0	4.8	7.8
1966	1	1	50%	14.5	4.4	5.9
1967	1	1	50%	20.0	3.9	8.0
1968	6	2	75%	24.2	4.5	8.1
CAREER	153	38	80.1%	15.1	4.7	5.4

REFERENCES

PRINT REFERENCES

Allen, Bob and Bill Gilbert. *The 500 Home Run Club*. Champaign, IL.: Sports Publishing Inc. 2000.

Allen, Maury. *Memories of the Mick*. Dallas: Taylor Publishing Company. 1997.

Anderson, Dave. "I'll Try to Make Up For Stuff." *New York Times* 12 July 1995: B9.

"All-Star Game Tickets Put On Sale by Yanks." *New York Times* 10 July 1960: S3.

Baseball Hall of Fame. *Baseball As America: Seeing Ourselves Through Our National Game*. Washington, D.C. National Geographic Society. 2002.

Beckett, Dr. James. *Mickey Mantle-Beckett Greatest Sports Heroes*. New York: House of Collectibles, Trademark of Random House. 1995.

Berger, Phil. *Mickey Mantle*. New York: Random House Value Publishing Inc. 1998.

Briordy, William J. "Mantle Heads Both Leagues in Homers, Runs Batted In and Batting Percentage; Yankee Finishes with .353 Mark; Mantle, in Pinch Role, Drives in Run as Bombers Lose to Red Sox in 10th, 7-4." *New York Times* 1 October 1956: 33.

Canale, Larry. *Mickey Mantle: The Classic Photo of Ozzie Sweet*. Richmond, Virginia: Tuff Stuff Publications. 1998.

Castro, Tony. Mickey Mantle: America's Prodigal Son. Washington D.C.: Brassey's Inc. 2002.

Creamer, Robert. *Mantle Remembered*. New York: Time Warner Books. 1995.

Creamer, Robert. *The Quality of Courage*. University of Nebraska: Bison Books. 1994.

Daley, Arthur. "Sports of the Times: Among the Missing." *New York Times* 8 April 1951:160.

Daley, Arthur. "Sports of the Times: An Afternoon at the Stadium; Bewildered Bystander No Help From Steve; The Green Peas." *New York Times* 18 April 1951: 53.

Daley, Arthur. "Sports of the Times: The Pause That Refreshes; Proving His Point; The Nose Knows Different Moisture. *New York Times* 9

October 1957: 56.

Daley, Arthur. "Another for the Nationals." *New York Times*. 14 July 1960: 30.

Dawson, James P. "Three Yankee Rookies Likely to Remain; A Candidate for the Clipper's Berth." *New York Times* 25 March 1951: 129.

Dawson, James P. "Twenty three Hits Top El Paso, 16-10; Draft Board Summons to Mantle; Rookie Ordered to Report for Re-Examination." *New York Times* 5 April 1951: 38.

Drebinger, John. "Yanks Blank Red Sox in First Game Before 44,860; Raschi and Jensen Spark 5-0 Triumph. Yankee Ace Holds Red Sox to 6 Singles." *New York Times* 18 April 1951:51.

Drebinger, John. "Dodgers Defeat Yankees in the 11th; Lead Series, 3-2." *New York Times* 5 October 1952: 1.

Drebinger, John. "Yanks Take Fifth Series in Row; Martin's Hit in Ninth Beats Dodgers, 4-3; Furillo's Last-Inning Homer Ties Score." *New York Times* 6 October 1953: 1.

Drebinger, John. "Mantle Hits Two Out of Washington Park as Yanks Drub Senators." *New York Times* 18 April 1956: 36.

Drebinger, John. "White Sox' Pierce Bows in 11th, 3-2; Mantle's Pennant-Winning Homer Enables Ford of Yanks to Win No. 19." *New York Times* 19 September 1956: 42.

Drebinger, John. "Mantle's Home Run and Bauer's Single Send Maglie to 2-0 Loss; Larsen Beats Dodgers in Perfect Game; Yanks Lead, 3-2, on First Series No-Hitter." *New York Times* 9 October 1956: 1.

Drebinger, John. "Kubek Sets Pace; Belts Two Homers for Yanks for 4 Runs Against Braves; Buhl is routed 12-3." *New York Times* 6 October

1957: 205.

Drebinger, John. "Braves Top Yanks in 10th Inning, 7-5 for Series 2-2 Tie; Mathews' Two-Run Homer Wins After Bombers Gain Lead on Bauer's

Triple; Howard Gets 4-Bagger, Connects With Two on in 9th to Deadlock Game." *New York Times* 7 October 1957, p.1.

Drebinger, John. "Burdette Hurls 7-Hit Shutout in 7th Game for his Third Victory; Braves Win, 5-0 and Take Series. *New York Times* 11 October

1957: 1

Drebinger, John. "Mays Stands Out in 6-0 Contest; Has a Homer, Two Singles and Stolen Base for Nationals, Who Use Twenty Six Players."

New York Times 14 July 1960: 30.

Drebinger, John. "Pirates Win, 10-9, Capturing Series on Homer in 9th; Mazeroski Hit Beats Yanks." *New York Times* 14 October 1960: 1.

Durso, Joseph. "Mantle Takes $100,000 Jersey Casino Job; Kuhn Orders Him to Sever Yankee Ties." *New York Times* 9 February 1983: B15.

Dylan, Bob. *Chronicles, Volume 1.* New York: Simon & Schuster. 2004.

Effrat, Louis. "Kucks Victor, 4-1 On Three Homers; Mantle Connects Twice and Carey Clouts 2-Run Blow for Yanks at Detroit; 47,756 See Game;

Stengel Hails Mantle." *New York Times* 21 June 1956: 51.

Effrat, Louis. "What a Change Mantle Hath Wrought in Fans; Those Who Used to Jeer Now Cheer Bronx Bombers; Oklahoma Kid Wins Friend for Yanks With Home Runs." *New York Times* 22 June 1956: 26.

Effrat, Louis. "Bombers Face Prospect of Losing Mantle for Fifth Series Contest; Shoulder Injury Handicap to Star." *New York Times* 7 October 1957: 31.

Effrat, Louis. "Bomber Suffer 5-4, 6-3 Setbacks; Senators Win in 15th After Grand Slam by Pascual Decides First Game." *New York Times* 15 August 1960: 27.

Effrat, Louis. "Ditmar 4-3 Victor with Five-Hitter; Pitcher Posts 12th Triumph -- Mantle Clouts Drive in All of Yankee Runs." New York Times 16 August 1960: 32.

Falkner, David. *The Last Hero: The Life of Mickey Mantle*. New York: Simon & Shuster. 1995.

Forker, Dom. *Sweet Seasons*. Texas: Taylor Publishing Company. 1990.

Frommer, Harvey. *The New York Yankee Encyclopedia*. New York: Macmillan. 1997.

Gallagher, Mark. *Explosion: Mickey Mantle Legendary Home Runs*. New York: Arbor House Publishing. 1987.

Gallagher, Mark and Walter LeConte. *The Yankee Encyclopedia*. Kingston, New York: Sports Publishing. 1997.

Gluck, Herb and Mickey Mantle. *The Mick*. New York: Doubleday & Company, Inc. 1985.

Golenbock, Peter. *Dynasty*. Upper Saddle River, New Jersey: Prentice-Hall. 2000.

Gould, Stephen Jay. *Full House: The Spread of Excellence From Plato to Darwin*. California: Three Rivers Press: January, 1997.

Hageman, William and Warren Wilbert. *New York Yankees: Seasons of Glory*.

New York: Jonathan David Publishers, Inc. 2001.

Halberstam, David. *October, 1964*. New York: Random House. 1995

Herskowitz, Mickey. *A Hero All His Life: A Memoir by the Mantle Family*. New York: Harper Collins. 1996.

Herskowitz, Mickey. *All My Octobers*. New York: Harper Collins. 2006.

Herskowitz, Mickey. *Mickey Mantle*. New York: William Morrow & Company. 1995.

Herskowitz, Mickey, David Mantle & Danny Mantle. *Mickey Mantle: Stories and Memorabilia from a Lifetime With the Mick*. New York: HNA Publishing. 2006.

Kubek, Tony &Terry Pluto. *Sixty-One*. New York: MacMillan Publishing Company. 1987.

Liederman, Bill and Maury Allen. *Our Mickey*. Chicago: Triumph Books. 2004.

"Look What I Got, Kids: Boy Takes Home Run Ball to Mazeroski; Gets to Keep It." *New York Times* 14 October 1960: 37.

Mantle, Mickey, Lewis Early, and Douglas A. MacKey. *Mickey Mantle: The American Dream Comes to Life*. Champaign, IL: Sagamore Publishing. 1994.

McGowen, Roscoe. "No Cut in Salary for Bomber Star; Same Contract as in 1950 to Be Sent to DiMaggio Next Week; Yankees Reveal Club Looks to Future, Sees Possible Replacement for Center Fielder in Mickey Mantle of Binghamton." *New York Times* 6 January 1951: 24.

McGowen, Roscoe. "Bankhead and Erskine Accept Dodger Terms for Total of Seventeen in Fold; Mantle Top Prospect." *New York Times* 21

January 1951: 139.

Meyerson, Allen B. "A Recovering Mantle is Vowing Amends." *New York*

Times 12 July 1995: B10.

"Boudreau Aligns a "Mantle Shift;" First Baseman Only Fielder to Hold Normal Station Against Yankee Star." *New York Times* 6 June 1956: 40.

Nuttall, David. *Mickey Mantle's Greatest Hits.* New York: S.P.I. Books. 1998.

Schoor, Gene. *The Illustrated History of Mickey Mantle.* New York: Carroll & Graff Publishers. 1996.

Sheehan, Joseph M. "Bombers' 5 Boots Mark 7-4 Setback; Four Unearned Tallies Help Kansas City Win." *New York Times* 6 June 1956: 40.

Sheehan, Joseph M. "Mantle Hits 19th and 20th Homers to Help Yankees Defeat Senators Twice; Bombers Record 4-3, 12-5 Verdicts. Mantle's First Game Homer 18 Inches Short of Going Over Roof at Stadium." *New York Times* 31 May 1956: 30.

Sheehan, Joseph M. "Mantle Wallops Two Homers to Help Top Athletics, 5-2." *New York Times* 6 May 1956: 193.

"Shortstop is Fit, Specialist Finds; Mantle Tested for Army." *New York Times* 12 April 1951: 51.

Smith, Ron and Billy Crystal. *61*: The Story of Roger Maris & Mickey Mantle and One Magical Summer.* St. Louis: *The Sporting News*, Vulcan Print Media Inc. 2001.

Smith, Marshall and Jim Rohle. *Memories of Mickey Mantle: My Very Best Friend.* Bronxville, New York: Adventure Quest Inc. 1996.

The All-Century Team. New York: Major League Baseball. 1999.

The Friends & Fans of Mickey Mantle. *Letters to Mickey.* New York: Harper Collins Publishers. 1995.

Williams, Ted, and John Underwood. *The Science of Hitting.* New York: Fireside Books. 1986.

WORLD WIDE WEBSITES

"1956 American League." *Baseball-Reference*. 5 July 2006 <Reference.com <http://www.baseball-reference.com/leagues/AL_1956.shtml>

"All-Star Game." *Major League Baseball*. 11 January 2007. <http://mlb.mlb.com/NASApp/mlb/mlb/history/all_star_event.jsp?story=1>

"Ardizoia, Rugger." *Baseball-Almanac*. 13 December 2006 <http://www.baseball-almanac.com/players/player.php?p=ardizru01>

"Barry Halper Dies at 66." *ESPN*. 3 February 2007. <http://sports.espn.go.com/espn/print?id=2265127&type=story>

"Carl Furillo." *Baseball Library*. 11 November 20, 2006. <http://www.baseballlibrary.com/baseballlibrary/ballplayers/F/Furillo_Carl.stm>

Dirks, Tim. "The Last Picture Show (1971)." *Filmsite*. 18 January 2007. http://www.filmsite.org/lastp.html

Early, Lewis. "Mickey Quotes." *The Mick*. 10 October 2006. <http://www.themick.com/mickeyquotes.htm>

"Ebbets Field." *Ballparks*. 11 September 2006.

<http://www.ballparks.com/baseball/national/ebbets.htm>

Friend, Harold. "A Costly Party: What a Difference a Martin Could Make." *BaseballLibrary*. 24 29 July 2006.

<http://www.baseballlibrary.com/baseballlibrary/submit/Friend_Harold6.stm>

Goldstein, Aaron. "The Extraordinary Life of Mel Allen." *The American Daily*. 6 May 2006. <http://americandaily.com/article/7424>

Green, Michelle. "Stephen Jay Gould: Driven By a Hunger to Learn and to Write." *The Unofficial Stephen Jay Gould Archive*. 13 December 2006. <http://www.stephenjaygould.org/library/green_sjgould.html>

"Home Run Records by a Team in a Single Season." *Baseball-Almanac*. 7 December 2006. <http://www.baseball-almanac.com/recbooks/rb_hr7.shtml>.

"Horse Racing." *Horseracing.About*. 15 January 2007. <http://horseracing.about.com/library/blroberto.htm>

Keene, Kerry. "The Last Pure Season: Review." *Baseball-Almanac*. 7 December 2006. <http://www.baseball-almanac.com/dugout01.shtml>

"Lew Burdette." *Baseball-Reference*. 12 June 2006.<http://www.baseball-reference.com/b/burdele01.shtml>

"Loews Regency Hotel" *Loews Hotels.* 20 August 2006.
<http://www.loewshotels.com/hotels/newyork/>

"Mantle was First in Fans' Hearts" *ESPN.* 20 August 2006.

<http://espn.go.com/sportscentury/features/00016135.html>

"Mel Ott." *The Baseball Page.* 2 January 2007.

<http://www.thebaseballpage.com/players/ottme01.php>

"Mickey Mantle. *Baseball Library.* 11 September 2006.

<http://www.baseballlibrary.com/ballplayers/player.php?name=Mickey_Mant
le_1931>

"Mickey Mantle." *Baseball-Reference."* 11 September 2006.
<http://www.baseball-reference.com/m/mantlmi01.shtml.>

"Mickey Mantle Quotes." *Baseball-Almanac.* 23 November
2006.<http://www.baseball-almanac.com/quotes/quomant.shtml>

"Mickey Mantle, Legend of Baseball, Dies at 63." Baseball-Almanac. 3
January 2007.

<http://www.baseball-almanac.com/deaths/mickey_mantle_obituary.shtml>

"Mickey_Mantle." *Wikipedia, the free encyclopedia.* 18 Dec2006.

Reference.com <http://www.reference.com/browse/wiki/Mickey_Mantle>

"Official Rules." *Major League Baseball.* 18 July 2006.
<http://mlb.mlb.com/NASApp/mlb/mlb/official_info/official_rules/definitio
n_terms_2.jsp>

Polo Grounds. *Ballparks.* 2 January 2007.
<http://www.ballparks.com/baseball/index.htm>

"Postseason 1955." *Baseball-Reference.* September 2006.<http://www.baseball-
reference.com/postseason/1955_WS.shtml>

"Red Smith Award." *Baseball-Almanac.* 7 December 2006.
<http://www.baseball-almanac.com/awards/aw_redsmith.shtml>

Ritter, Lawrence S. "A Classic of Cricket, a Legend of Baseball." *New York
Times* 25 March1984. 7 December 2006, p. BR1.
<http://query.nytimes.com/gst/fullpage.html?res=9C02E6DB1039F936A15
750C0A962948260>

"Rocky Colavito." *Baseball-Reference.* 5 June 2006.<http://www.baseball-
reference.com/c/colavro01.shtml>

"Rocky Colavito." *BaseballLibrary.* 5 June 2006.
<http://www.baseballlibrary.com/baseballlibrary/ballplayers/C/Colavito_Roc
ky.stm>

Romano, John. "Baseball Adopts a New Zone." *St. Petersburg Times*. 27 February 2001. 1 August 2006 <http://www.sptimes.com/News/022701/Sports/Baseball_adapts_to_a_.shtml>

"Sain, John." *Baseball Reference*.12 June 2006. <http://www.baseball-reference.com/s/sainjo01.shtml>

"Seasons for the Ages. 1961: Chasing the Babe." *The Sporting News*. 2 February 2007.

http://archive.sportingnews.com/baseball/al100/seasons/1961.html

Schechter, Gabriel. "Mickey Mantle's 1956 Triple Crown Season." *Baseball Hall of Fame*. 15 January 2007. <http://www.baseballhalloffame.org/history/2006/061120.htm>

"Strike Zone." *Answers*. 2 August 2006 <http://www.answers.com/topic/strike-zone>

Schwartz, Larry. "He Was First in Fan's Hearts." *ESPN*. 22 November 2006.

<http://espn.go.com/sportscentury/features/00016135.html>

Shimidzu, Kadzuwo J. Ed. "A Triviana of Oh, Sadaharu, The World's All-Time Home Run King." 7 December 2006.

<http://homepage3.nifty.com/kadzuwo/triviana/oh.htm>

Smith, David. *Retrosheet*. 1 May 2006.<http://www.retrosheet.org/>

"Willie Mays." *The Baseball Library*. 12 January 2007.

<http://www.baseballlibrary.com/baseballlibrary/ballplayers/M/Mays_Willie.stm>

"Willie's Farewell." *Time Magazine*. 12 January 2007.
<http://www.time.com/time/magazine/article/0,9171,946373,00.html>

Wulf, Steve. "Superman in Pinstripes. Mickey Mantle 1931-1995." *Time Magazine*. 23 November 2006.
<http://www.time.com/time/magazine/article/0,9171,134580,00.html>

Purchase other Black Rose Writing titles at www.blackrosewriting.com/books
and use promo code PRINT to receive a 20% discount.

Made in the USA
Middletown, DE
08 August 2017